THE OT

THE
OTHER YOU

HOW TO DEVELOP YOUR PSYCHIC POTENTIAL

Andrew Laurance

JAVELIN BOOKS
POOLE · NEW YORK · SYDNEY

First published in the UK 1986 by Javelin Books,
Link House, West Street, Poole, Dorset, BH15 1LL

Copyright © 1986 Andrew Laurance

Distributed in the United States by
Sterling Publishing Co., Inc.,
2 Park Avenue, New York, NY 10016

Distributed in Australia by
Capricorn Link (Australia) Pty Ltd,
PO Box 665, Lane Cove, NSW 2066.
ISBN 0 7137 1719 X

British Library Cataloguing in Publication Data

Laurence, Andrew
  The other you: how to develop your paranormal
  potential.
  1. Psychical research
  I. Title
  133.8   BF1031

Typeset by Poole Typesetting (Wessex) Ltd.

Printed in Great Britain by Guernsey Press, Guernsey, C.I.

CONTENTS

INTRODUCTION

It is an undeniable fact that astonishing breakthroughs are being made in psychic fields which cannot but fascinate everyone, however much the whole business of the paranormal may be regarded as a subject best left to lunatics.

One of the reasons why the possible psychic development of man has been neglected by respected scientists, and ignored by the more forward thinking tycoons as not being worth analytical or financial investigation, is that research into the supernatural is time consuming, expensive and, at present, totally unrewarding.

Revelations that 'A' has been able to communicate with 'B' five feet away by telepathy, or that 'K' can move a match-stick three millimetres on a marble table by sheer willpower, hardly capture the imagination.

If our dormant telepathic powers were fully unleashed, however, it might well cause chaos in the money markets. The telephone network would suffer, newspaper sales would plummet because everyone would know what is happening before it happens, and few would watch television because programmes would be foreseen before they were even produced.

As to psychokinesis (the ability to move objects at the touch of a brainwave) transport contractors would feel the draught as consumer products were sent from one city to another on the nod of a manufacturer versed in the supernatural, or whole households moved across country at the wink of a psychically astute removals man.

But we are by no means there yet, so a study of how we are advancing in these areas, without bias and ignoring what the sceptics can too easily put down, seems worthwhile.

I think it essential from the outset to explain why I have written this book and who I have written it for.

I am, by profession, a novelist, a writer of fiction, and therefore understandably suspect, but since it has been said often enough that fact is stranger than fiction, I have set out to spotlight the unnerving things which have been done in the paranormal fields that are too extraordinary to be considered merely coincidence, and also to suggest what can still be done to broaden our vision and experiences.

My interest in psychic phenomena, which led to the belief that we all have it in us to develop untapped powers of perception, started over fifteen years ago when my publishers suggested I should write a 'psychic thriller'.

It was a completely new area of thought as far as I was concerned for, apart from having had my fortune told once or twice, I had till then taken little interest in such things.

The Tarots, however, were as good a starting point as any and the first thriller I launched myself into embraced predictions, premonitions and forebodings. The research that this drew me into swept me down diverse currents of the paranormal so quickly that I was not only immersed in the opaque sea of the mysterious to the point of drowning, but was soon made to realize that I had to avoid swimming towards the wilder shores of the unexplained if I was to retain my sanity.

It seemed to me imperative to eliminate that which had no foundation in this life as we know it, to discard the past and only look to the future, but my first real attempt at making contact with my other self was so haunted by the dead, that I realized I would have to spend some time finding out more about the bag of history we all carry around with us, and how this influences our attitudes, before moving on to the more scientific experiments which prove we can be more than we at present are.

I am therefore addressing myself to the curious and those, perhaps, who need reassuring that they are not wasting their time prodding the esoteric.

The religious, who have no difficulty in believing the incredible because they have been taught not to doubt, should find no surprises, but they are unlikely to open the pages that follow as their teachings warn them against anything not contained in their own particular holy books.

Those who dabble with spiritualism or flirt with black magic and witchcraft will certainly be disappointed, for there is nothing in this volume that is not in the end firmly rooted in this earth, in this life, or within ourselves.

The chapters of this book are set out in the sequence in which I tackled each subject in my researches, and what they led me to, the experiences I had, those of others and what can be expected.

I am not psychic. I do not have special powers that other people cannot develop. What I do have, is a completely open mind and the belief that all of us have it in us to awaken dormant senses and expand those of which we are aware, providing we bother to observe our own behaviour and jettison, from the very beginning, the obsession that strange happenings are only coincidence.

We should all try to develop the supernatural slant in ourselves. No harm, after all, can come of it and, if we succeed in travelling through space, in reading other people's thoughts, it could result in some quite astonishing repercussions – political, financial and environmental.

There is a superbeing in all of us.
It is just a matter of working hard to find him.

1
BREAKING THROUGH

Any attempt to better oneself, whether mentally or physically, can be thwarted from the start by outside influences: friends and relations may tell you that what you want to achieve is impossible, ridiculous, beyond your capabilities, that you need incredible patience when you have none, will-power which you totally lack, or health and strength that you don't possess.

The very first step in striving for a supernatural state, therefore, is to isolate yourself completely from other people's opinions, and the best way to do that is not tell anyone what you are doing.

The second step is to get yourself in the right frame of mind to accept as reality those things which you have been taught are fantasy.

And the third step is to prove to your own satisfaction, from the very beginning, that *another you* does exist.

Discovering this takes time.

Recognizing it takes longer.

Making contact with it is the breakthrough.

There are several methods of reaching out for the other self, the simplest of which in theory happens to be most difficult in practice, for it is like trying to balance a small drop of mercury along the edge of a matchstick. It can be done but it takes time.

THE MIRROR METHOD

All you have to do is stand in front of a mirror and stare at your own reflection until you no longer recognize yourself but see another individual, with the same familiar features as yourself, the same expressions, but somehow he or she has become meaningless.

After a short time you will have this sensation but you will quickly lose it. You will move a hand, a foot, you will blink more than is necessary, and this other person will become you being stupid with yourself. You will need to pull a face perhaps, grimace, blow out your cheeks, just to make sure that you are in control of yourself, and it is in this fraction of a second when this need to confirm your existence becomes urgent, that you are discovering the 'other you'.

It is an unnerving moment and far more difficult to hang on to than one might suppose, but regular practice at staring at oneself in the mirror, especially in the eyes, will eventually enable you to recognize the 'feeling of another you', the sensation that there is another awareness within you that is never consciously used.

When you are capable of looking at your reflection in any mirror, whether in private or when people are around you, and make immediate contact with the other self, and you find the sensation gives you confidence, you have taken the very first step towards believing that there is more within you than you supposed and in understanding that the very centre of your being – the inner core that controls everything you do – is also in control of the other you and has been since the day you were born – or even before.

When you first make contact with your other self you may feel extremely uncomfortable. I have previously used the word 'unnerving' because that is exactly what it should be. If that second of recognition is so unbearable that you feel you would rather not repeat the experiment, not face the fact that there is another you, I would suggest that you persevere and dare yourself to go on, for it is this very sensation of being unnerved that is the moment of truth – and therefore extremely precious.

The ability to make contact with, and hold onto, your second personality will eventually come more and more easily, by which time it will be similar to summoning the presence of a new friend, blood brother or sister, extremely exhilarating and comforting as you will know that they will for ever be loyal.

In order to consolidate this new relationship and determine what your capabilities in the paranormal fields might be, three further experiments should be tried.

THE TAROT METHOD
The first of these is to contact the other you using the Tarot cards.

It involves no one else and comes down to telling your own fortune, not to find out what your future will be – which is sometimes possible – but to get a reaction from your subconscious.

Tarot cards are available from any reputable bookstore or stationers; they can be regarded as simple playing cards or a psychological calculator which will give you random answers to random questions.

The Tarots first appeared in Europe in the fourteenth century and were used by Spanish gypsies. They were the ancestors of the playing cards with which we play bridge, canasta and poker today, but they were also regarded as a phenomenon, for in any literature that recognizes the existence of hidden knowledge, the Tarots are always mentioned as a major influence.

There are a number of variations on the Tarot pack, but the 'Tarot de Marseilles', consisting of 78 cards, is considered by most occultists to represent its oldest form.

There are four suits – Cups (Hearts), Pentacles (Diamonds), Wands (Clubs), and Swords (Spades).

There are 56 ordinary playing cards, as opposed to 52 in modern packs, four additional Knights being added between the Queens and the Knaves. This set is known as the Lesser Arkana.

The Greater Arkana, quite separate and not suited, consists of 22 specially named and numbered cards, not used in normal play but potent in occult portent.

All the cards have different designs, each of which is heavily symbolic, and by dealing them out in various ways, insight into the past, present and future of a querent's character and motivation can be read by those who know how.

The pack of Tarots is said to represent an Egyptian hieroglyphic book originally found in the form of 78 large clay tablets, later reproduced in wood, in metal and then paper. It has always been believed that this book contains certain philosophical and psychological interpretations. Doubts that this is true, and the idea that the book was first devised by calculating occultists, not by gypsies who made up the story as part of a sales pitch, can be gleaned if one studies just one of the many complicated meanings handed down through history.

If the pack is divided into three parts it can represent the 'other you' enveloped by the psychic shield which protects it from the everyday physical world which surrounds it.

The 'other you' is represented by the Greater Arkana card zero which is placed in the centre of a triangle (the Trinity?) made up of the remaining 21 Greater Arkana cards, seven cards to each side of the triangle. The triangle is then surrounded by a square, the 56 Lesser Arkana cards, 14 cards to each side of the square.

By placing the Tarots in this setting on a table and staring at them, the mind will start associating itself with the feeling that a great deal of thought has gone into each separate design. I would not go as far as suggesting that their magical properties will be felt instantly, because we do not live in a world where magic comes easily to mind, but the ritual will help break such down to earth thoughts as 'I only bought these bits of cardboard at the stationers round the corner last week – how can they mean anything?'

14

The Tarots, when first trying to contact the 'other you', should be used to awaken your ability to perceive your subconscious.

The individual cards and the language of their meaning accustom the mind to think differently, to think in another dimension, with wider concepts which break down inhibitions.

There are countless methods of divination using the Tarots, and it is beyond the scope of this book to give them all, as it is to itemise the meaning of each card. All Tarot packs are now sold with a small booklet explaining divinatory meanings and methods and there are a great number of books available on this subject. I have found the clearest to be *The Pictorial Key to the Tarot*, by A.E. Waite and it is using his references that I set out below a simple and quick method of divination using only the Greater Arkana.

This method relates to a specific problem which troubles you and to which you would like a solution, and you should bear it in mind as you shuffle the pack.

If you are relaxed and tired it seems that the recognition of what the cards suggest comes more easily to you, as the interpretation of dreams is easier to understand on just awakening.

Reading the Tarot
Having shuffled the 22 Greater Arkana cards, you should slide the top card off and place it face down on a table in front of you. It is important that the card should at all times be placed as it comes off the pack as a reversed or upside down card can have a different meaning to one that is the right way up.

Shuffle the cards again, slide off the second card and place it to the *left* of the 1st.

Shuffle the cards again and slide off the third card, placing it to the *right* of the first.

Shuffle the cards again and slide off the fourth card, placing it *above* the first.

Shuffle the cards again and slide off the fifth card, placing it *below* the first.

You now have the cards before you in the shape of a cross.

Turn them over one by one, as though you were turning over the page of a book, and read off their divinatory meanings.

The first card is the significator and will set the mood of the reading in relation to the problem you are hoping to solve.

The second card represents the forces working in favour of you finding a solution.

The third card represents the forces working against you finding a solution.

The fourth card represents the direction from which you may get help to solve the problem.

The fifth card will give you one possible solution.

Each card, however, has several alternative meanings, and it is in deciding which meaning in relation to the other cards is the most relevant, that you will achieve a satisfactory reading and an insight as to how you can be guided by what seems to be an external power but which, in fact, is simply the other you.

Below I give you two readings which I carried out when I tried to contact my other self.

The first problem I wished to solve was the straightforward one of whether I should purchase a certain house or not.

The second problem was whether I believed deep down that 'another me' existed.

The meanings are taken from the A.E. Waite book published at the same time as a new set of cards created by the medium Pamela Colman Smith in 1910. They are, together with the 'Tarot de Marseilles' regarded as the most authentic pack.

First reading
Question: Should I purchase the house I viewed yesterday?
Feelings: I liked the house but am not sure it is right for the family.
1   SIGNIFICATOR   *The Chariot.*
    Succour, providence; also war, triumph, presumption, vengeance, trouble.

2   FORCES IN FAVOUR   *The Tower*. (Reversed).
Oppression, imprisonment, tyranny, deception, ruin, distress in lesser degrees.

3   FORCES AGAINST   *The Star*. (Reversed).
Arrogance, haughtiness, impotence.

4   SOLUTION COMING FROM   *The Hermit*.
Prudence, circumspection; also treason, roguery, complete dissimulation.

5   POSSIBLE SOLUTION   *The Fool*.
Folly, mania, extravagance, intoxication, delirium, frenzy.

Of the alternatives of *The Chariot* – the SIGNIFICATOR, Succour and Trouble were the two words I immediately reacted to. The idea of moving at all was to help the family situation. The reading would have to bear this in mind. Would the house help the situation or not?

'Oppression' and 'Imprisonment' were the words I instinctively reacted to for the FORCES IN FAVOUR. *The Tower* is a destructive card which seemed to be telling me that my reason for moving was that I felt 'oppressed' and 'imprisoned' where I was. The 'arrogance' of the FORCES AGAINST in *The Star* (Reversed) leapt out at me. I clearly liked the house because it looked impressive and was in an up-market and snobby area. This rather stark home-truth jarred.

Of the alternatives on *The Hermit*, the DIRECTION OF THE POSSIBLE SOLUTION, 'prudence' was obvious. I had felt this all the time, but who likes to be prudent? and then *The Fool* gave me the SOLUTION. The card spoke for itself, 'extravagance' standing out with bright lights flashing.

Not believing for one moment that some magical powers within the cards, or their spirit or anything which might smack of witchcraft, had anything to do with the clear message, I decided against purchasing that particular house because the thoughts stimulated by the reading clarified my doubts, subconscious doubts which my emotional 'arrogance' had been cleverly clouding.

Second reading

Question: Does an 'other me' exist?

Feelings: If I did not have doubts I would not seek an answer.

1   SIGNIFICATOR   *Justice* (Reversed)
    Law in all its departments, legal complications, bigotry, bias, excessive severity.

2   FORCES IN FAVOUR   *High Priestess*
    Secrets, the future as yet unrevealed, silence. Tenacity, mystery, wisdom, science.

3   FORCES AGAINST   *The Sun*
    Material happiness. Fortunate marriage. Contentment.

4   SOLUTION COMING FROM   *The Hanged Man*.
    Wisdom, circumspection, trials, sacrifice, intuition, discretion, prophecy.

5   POSSIBLE SOLUTION   *The Last Judgement*.
    Change of position. Renewal. Outcome.

I was heartened by this reading which felt good from the start.

Of the alternatives of *Justice* (Reversed) the SIGNIFICATOR, 'Excessive severity' struck me as important, reading it as severity against my own bigotry and bias.

With this in mind, I found all the alternatives for *The High Priestess*, FORCES IN FAVOUR, totally acceptable, and the alternatives for the FORCES AGAINST in *The Sun* quite understandable as my fears of losing material happiness, a fortunate marriage and contentment were upset by my isolation if I found the 'other me'.

A POSSIBLE SOLUTION COMING FROM *The Hanged Man* as wisdom, discernment, trials (experiments?) sacrifices, intuition, divination and prophecy all pointed incredibly in the direction I wanted – and *wanted* was the key word emerging from my other self, confirmed by a SOLUTION from *The Last Judgement*, its 'change of position' striking me as advice rather than an answer.

The Tarot readings give so many clever alternatives that it could be said they can never be wrong. The querent will always find the solution he wants.

This, in part, is true. But the querent, more often than not, has no idea what he wants. When forced to make a choice between the alternatives, he discovers what he wants but, I believe, is only shocked into this realization by choices he never considered.

A comparison can be made with someone who is hungry, sitting down at a restaurant table not knowing what he wants to eat. The description of alternative dishes leaping out at him from the menu makes the mouth water, and a choice is made. Fish was thought of, but not grilled dover sole. Meat was considered, but not peppered steak. The menu awakens the taste buds, as the Tarots awaken the 'other you'.

THE OUIJA OR PLANCHETTE METHOD

The second experiment to try in order to make contact with your other self might be said to have shades of sorcery. But like the Tarots it must be remembered that it is used purely as a stepping stone to get the mind working in directions it is not used to.

Mention of the ouija or planchette can bring accusations that you are trying to contact spirits of the past or the future. Devils, demons and goodness knows what. But the ouija is nothing of the sort, though it does produce a powerful and mysterious force best explained as a form of electromagnetism. In my novel 'Ouija', the opening paragraph reads thus:

'All you need is a polished surface, the alphabet laid out in a circle and a tumbler,' she explained. 'Then you place a finger on the base of the inverted glass and it moves from letter to letter spelling out a message.'

'From whom?'

'From the dead.'

This, of course, is pure fantasy.

There is no skullduggery about the ouija, it is simply a way of getting messages from your own or other people's subconscious, though this may result in unsettling, embarrassing and sometimes obscene ideas coming through.

The word ouija is derived from the French *oui* and the German *ja*, proclaiming the affirmative when asking if it is possible to make contact with another world.

Its origin dates back to the fourth century AD when a pendulum was used, a weight on the end of a piece of string swinging above the letters of the alphabet towards certain letters spelling out words and phrases.

In Victorian times the ouija board came into its own as a family game. This consisted of a flat piece of highly polished wood on which were engraved the letters of the alphabet in a semi-circle. Over this a smaller triangular shaped piece of wood on mini-casters moved from letter to letter when finger tips were placed on it.

The ouija principle is called planchette when a pencil actually writes out letters of messages; this is a far more elaborate device and comes into the realms of automatic writing.

The ouija certainly has a history of mystery. The criticism that one or more of the querents are pushing the glass is so obvious that it seems infantile to suggest it, considering the experiment's popularity as a game over the years, but the power that moves the glass from letter to letter, sometimes quite violently, can be as frightening as it is incomprehensible.

Sir William Barrett (1845-1926), Professor of Physics at the Dublin Royal College of Science tried to fathom out the ouija and carried out tests by first shuffling the letters of the alphabet around each time a new question was asked, in order to confuse whoever might be pushing the glass, then turned the letter cards over so that no one could guess which one was which. This made no difference. Understandable messages still came through.

In his *Autobiography*, published posthumously, G.K. Chesterton, wrote on the ouija:

> I saw quite enough of the thing to be able to testify, with complete certainty, that something happens which is not in the ordinary sense natural, or produced by the normal and conscious human will. Whether it is produced by some subconscious but still human force, or

by some powers, good, bad or indifferent, which are external to humanity I would not attempt to decide. The only thing I will say with complete confidence, about that mystic and invisible power, is that it tells lies.

Alan Vaughan in *Patterns of Prophecy* describes how, in 1965, he bought a ouija board to entertain a friend who was convalescing. They heard on the radio that a well-known journalist had died from a heart attack and consulted the ouija to find out if this was true. The ouija told them the journalist had actually died of poison.

Ten days later an inquest revealed that this was the true cause of death.

A group of four people sitting round a highly polished circular table using a lightweight crystal tumbler, has always brought the best results.

Letters from A to Z and numerals from 1 to 10 should be clearly written on separate cards, laid out in no particular order round the edge of the table and, to save time, a 'yes' card and a 'no' card should also be included.

A darkened room with not too bright a light over the table helps to create the right atmosphere, focussing the attention on the business in hand. Perhaps soft classical music in the background also helps everyone to relax.

One feels remarkably stupid asking a question out loud to no one in particular, and nervous giggles must be expected to begin with, but when the glass starts to move (all querents placing the very tips of their index fingers on the base of the upturned tumbler) usually in fits and starts, you will find that those present become totally involved.

I have experimented with the ouija many times and have had some quite outstanding results, the glass once moving so forcefully that it shot off the table from under my friends' fingers to shatter on the floor some distance across the room.

The most curious session I had was when I made contact with a lady who called herself Natalia and claimed to be the grand-mother of an Italian film producer who wanted me to write her life story so that he could make a film of it (of course). She addressed herself directly to me and asked me to contact her grandson, whose name was Carlatti, and tell him that she could not rest as she had been responsible for accusing her lover of having killed her husband when she herself had knifed him, in 1913. Great stuff. Not unlike a story I might have written, coupled with the wishful thinking of movie rights, which pointed to my subconscious at work.

Natalia, when asked, gave me her grandson's telephone number in Milan, and as soon as it was polite to do so, I left her and the session to ring him up.

The number rang but never answered.

I tried over a period of several weeks, and eventually got an 'unobtainable' tone. On enquiring I was informed that the number had been disconnected. I checked that it had once been that of a gentleman by the name of Carlatti, and was corrected. It was the number of a gentleman called Calvacanti, a film director who died in 1955.

Had I read it all somewhere? I think it very possible. But what I was unable to explain was a contact made during another session by my Spanish wife.

She was given a message from her dead father through the ouija not to worry about Sacrista. She had no idea who Sacrista was, indeed had never heard the name. But three days later her mother rang from Spain telling her, among other things, that her cousin, whom she might not remember, had died after a long illness. Her second name was Sacrista.

It sends a little chill down your spine when such things happen to you, but it can be explained if you accept that we are all at certain times in contact with each other through subconscious telepathy.

Out of four or five people sitting round a table for a ouija session, there will always be one who seems to be pushing the

22

glass more than others. You must accept that they are more highly sensitive than the rest and have no idea what they are doing, that they are to the ouija what a medium is to spiritualism.

If you do not trust them, ask them to abstain from the board for a while and you will find that the glass will go on moving without them, though probably a good deal less actively.

It is best to ask simple questions at first which can be answered with a 'yes' or 'no'.

Is anyone there? (always idiotic, but you have to start somewhere).

Are you alive?

Are you dead?

When did you die? (A numerical date).

What is your name? (Personalizing the messenger helps everyone to concentrate. A silly name invariably comes out with an unlikely history – the fantasies of the group subconscious. I once got a bald Red Indian called Sioux (original!) who wanted to scalp me.)

Have you got a message for someone round this table?

Who? (It gets hairy when the glass spells out the name of one of the assembled).

What is the message?

THE MEMORY METHOD

The third experiment worth trying in order to prove to yourself that there is a 'subconscious you' that can be brought out, is much less dramatic and requires plenty of time and a great deal of patience. Its aim is to reveal that there is, within you, a vast amount of knowledge of which you are unaware, and that within that bank of knowledge there may be something useful which will help you develop.

It is based on the, as yet unproven, theory that we inherit memory. Our features and characteristics, colour of hair, height, shape of nose, are handed down from generation to generation, and there seems to be no reason why memory should not also be inherited, for example, a vivid event experienced by one's grandfather, passed on down along with the shape of his forehead, his sense of humour, or his lack of it.

The first inkling I had that one might inherit memory was when I was reading a book by Colette, the French authoress, and came across a passage relating to a house in Neuilly in *Cheri* which I had never read before. I felt that eerie sensation that I had either been in that house or perhaps had read the passage somewhere before.

I happened to mention this to my grandmother who was quite astonished at what I had to say. She recalled the passage perfectly, for she had known Colette and had been in that particular house.

More recently I had another experience with my five year old daughter, when she reacted to a particular piece of music which I, as a young man, had loved. The piece was not played in isolation, but was part of an LP – Erroll Garner.

My daughter was playing on the floor while the first two numbers were blaring out. They had no particular effect on her, but when the third piece *Confessin'* started up, she immediately got to her feet to move to the rhythm.

She danced around for the rest of that number, then sat down to go on playing when it came to an end. The rest of the LP played on.

Why had she reacted to that particular number which I had played incessantly when I was younger?

I tried another experiment with her, using a whole spectrum of coloured crayons. Among them was a pink pencil and a green pencil; both particular shades of which reminded me of two toy cars I played with when I was about her age. These two particular colours have always remained significant for me. I react, with nostalgia, whenever they catch my eye, whether they are part of a dress pattern, a curtain design or the colour of a real car.

I asked my daughter to pick out her two favourite colours and she picked out the pink straight away, then a green one, though a different shade, more yellow than *my* favourite.

Coincidence, or inherited?

I was so fascinated by the possibility of our subconscious stacking up memories which might go back generations and generations, that I wrote an article for one of the national dailies requesting readers to send in their possible experiences.

Unfortunately, the newspaper headlined the article 'Phobias' and many of the letters that poured in concerned themselves with just that. However, there were three interesting examples of pure, inherited memory. The first, a woman who reacted strongly to the smell of burning rubber because her father (before she was born) was nearly incinerated in a fire at the rubber plant where he worked when it caught fire. The second was an artist who found himself oppressed when mixing a certain shade of red and found out that his father was nearly drowned in a yachting accident, trapped under a sail of that red colour when the yacht capsized. And third, the girl who instinctively became fearful regularly on Saturday nights at around 10.30 who eventually discovered that her grandparents ran a public house in a rough district of Glasgow, and that on Saturday nights they lived in fear of the violence that invariably erupted at closing time.

All this is to suggest that you should try to pick up on any *déjà vu* experiences – the feeling that you have been in a place before, that a particular event is not new – and check whether it is familiar to one of your parents, grandparents or indeed great-grandparents.

The *déjà vu* phenomenon is often said to be evidence of reincarnation, but inherited memory strikes me as a much more likely explanation.

If you happen to touch on such an experience, you will again feel that moment of awe about your own capabilities and it is this 'awe' for the infinite possibilities in your own subconscious that you must grab hold of with your mind and hold on to for as long as possible.

In the chapters that follow, ideas on various experiments are suggested. To achieve some degree of success it is vital that you should be in a state of total relaxation, in order to link both levels of mind, the conscious and the subconscious.

In most people there is a continual state of stress. To reduce this nervous tension, therefore, the following very simple exercise is advised.

Lie quietly in a dark room for five minutes and start to breathe in slowly counting to six; hold your breath for three seconds, exhale slowly on a count of six, then wait three seconds; breathe in again on a count of six, and so on.

When you have done this for about five minutes you will find most of the tension has gone.

2
TELEPATHY

. . .the communication of impressions of any kind from one mind to another, independently of the recognized channels of sense.

Oxford English Dictionary

How often do you think of someone out of the blue, decide to ring them up, and learn that they were about to ring you?

How many times have you been about to pick up the phone to ring someone and it has rung, and it is that very person on the other end of the line?

Do you make a note of such an occurrence? Or do you just shrug it off as coincidence, mentioning it perhaps to one or two people who aren't in the least bit interested, then forget all about it till the next time?

Why is it that we sometimes think of people suddenly, for no apparent reason? Is it because they are thinking about us? Who tries to find out? And *how* does one find out? For it is rather embarrassing to contact Tom, Dick or Harry, and ask whether they were thinking about you, unless, of course you sense such an element of anxiety at the time that you get hold of the person on some other pretext.

The most common examples of such straightforward telepathy are invariably linked with fear which generates powerful transmitting powers to the person who senses danger.

When one is afraid the body reacts chemically. In his book *Bodily Changes in Pain, Hunger, Fear and Rage*, the American physiologist W.B. Cannon explains that an emotional condition of extreme danger, aggression or defensiveness is controlled by the sympathetic nervous system.

The sympathetic nervous system acts as an antagonist in the body to the parasympathetic nervous system. What the one does, the other counteracts. The sympathetic speeds up the heartbeat, the parasympathetic slows it down. Sympathetic action causes the blood vessels to constrict and prepares the body for great exertion, while the parasympathetic causes blood vessels to dilate and therefore relaxes. The sympathetic causes the pupil to dilate, the parasympathetic causes the muscles of the pupil of the eye to constrict. The sympathetic in general causes inhibition, whereas the secretion of sweat and saliva and gastric gland juices is caused by the parasympathetic.

The sympathetic nervous system is activated by adrenalin and adrenalin related compounds. The dominance of the sympathetic nervous system is therefore known as adrenergia.

Andrija Puharich, the American neurologist, famous for his book *The Sacred Mushroom* and director of extrasensory perception studies in Maine, suggests in his work on telepathy (*Beyond Telepathy*) that persons dominated by adrenergia transmit telepathic messages subconsciously, while persons who are on the contrary very relaxed, become reliable receivers. As an example of this he relates the story of two colleagues who, subconsciously made extraordinary telepathic contact enabling one to save the life of the other.

In Boston, one day in 1955, a welder named Jack Sullivan was working in a deep trench on a new waterpipe system. Late in the afternoon, when the main pipe was laid, the power shovel crew stopped work leaving Jack to finish off the seaming.

Alone, intent on what he was doing, he was unaware of earth movements around him and was suddenly engulfed when the trench caved in.

Trapped by tons of rubble, mud and sand, he was virtually buried alive, his legs caught under his own weight, his head jammed in the welding mask, while his shoulders were pressed against the still red hot pipe he had welded.

Above him, unaware of what had happened because the generator was still on, the crew moved off, packing up for the day, happy to leave Jack on his own.

Jack's position forbade any movement. He suffered severe burns, but somehow managed to get his hand up above his head and, he hoped, out and above in the air where he waved it. At first he shouted, but knowing the noise of the generator would drown any other sounds, he decided to save his breath, preserve what little oxygen was available, in the belief that help was bound to come – if not immediately, at least in twenty-four hours when the crew returned. It was not a pleasant prospect, but a question of survival.

Preparing himself as best he could to see the night out, not wanting to contemplate death, not believing that such a stupid accident could end so fearfully, he started thinking of who would first miss him and perhaps put out an early alarm, when, for no explainable reason, a vivid picture of his colleague Tommy Whittaker, came to mind.

Whittaker was another welder working on a different section of the water main, some five miles away in Westwood. There was no reason why Whittaker should worry about Jack's absence, even if it was noticed. Jack had chosen to work on the Washington Street site only that morning, it had not been worked for several weeks and there was no reason why anyone on the Westwood team should be at all concerned.

However, the thought of Tommy Whittaker persisted in Jack's mind, so he contemplated on his friendship with this man, which had always been cordial, indeed fun.

Five miles away Whittaker was welding, much as Jack had been. As the work was mechanical, automatic and somewhat boring, his mind wandered a good deal while he watched the sparks fly and the red and blue hot seam coming together.

For no reason that he could explain to himself at the time, Whittaker started thinking about what was going on at the Washington Street site, and he got it into his mind that he should go there to see how work was progressing. There was no need for him to do so; to go there on his way home meant a good deal of twisting and turning to avoid the heavy traffic, but all the same he decided that when he had finished this particular part of the pipe he would get in his car and go there. Something was nagging him about the site, something was drawing him there.

On arrival at Washington Street, after getting stuck in rush hour jams, he pulled up beside the generator truck which was still humming, and looked around feeling that something was wrong.

He walked over to the newly re-laid trench, thought the job had been badly done, then realized that there had been a cave-in.

Seconds later he saw Jack Sullivan's hand, limply moving its fingers, and he called for help, and Jack was rescued.

Tommy Whittaker had been relaxed, bored by the mechanicalness of the welding he was doing and therefore in a perfect state of mind to receive a telepathic message.

Jack Sullivan, stressed to the extreme and under the threat of death, had massive adrenergia – the perfect state for sending out a telepathic message.

In 1984 a similar set of circumstances involved two brothers, Christopher and Michael Bentley who both lived together in London. One Saturday evening they were to meet up at a party in a Berkshire village. Christopher drove off first with his girl-friend. Michael followed later and went to collect his girl-friend from a North London flat, but she had fallen ill and was unable to join him so he drove alone. On the way he decided to take a short cut, got lost, then in a storm that came up skidded and crashed into a wall. The area was deserted, it was night; he panicked.

A few miles away, at the party in a country house, Christopher mellowed by the first drinks quite suddenly became concerned about his brother who was late and should have appeared. Against his friends' protests that he was worrying unduly, he got in his car to drive along the road back to London in the hope of meeting up with Michael.

Once alone, more relaxed, he actually stopped the car to consider what he was doing. If truth be known, he had left the party because he was rather bored, using Michael's absence as an excuse, but, for some inexplicable reason, he felt he needed to drive for a while in solitude, and he took the next turning on the left which, he knew, would eventually lead back to the party.

Half a mile or so along the lane his headlights picked out Michael walking towards him.

'I thought you'd find me,' Michael said, not particularly surprised.

'How? Why? I've never been down this road before, nor have you.'

'A gut feeling,' Michael retorted. 'We're probably in contact telepathically without knowing it.'

Which was indeed the case.

EXPERIMENTS IN TELEPATHY

The usual everyday examples of telepathy, however, are so mundane, that they occur without even the participants being aware of what is happening.

It is essential, therefore, for anyone trying to develop telepathic powers, to be aware of what comes into their minds at all times and to make notes, preferably in diary form, and *experiment*.

Solo one-way experiments are advised till some success has been achieved simply because so much patience is required that only you can judge how efficient you are being.

I tried one long telepathic experiment over a period of six weeks as a sender, never telling the receiver what I was actually doing.

31

I took advantage of the fact that the person, whom I shall call John was fascinated by dreams. I told him I was researching dreams and suggested that for the next few weeks he should have a notepad by his bed and write down the very first thing that came into his mind on first awakening.

I knew that during working days he woke at 7.30, I made sure that I woke some time before that and at 7.30 concentrated hard on thinking about him, coupled with an image – a tree, a dog, a cat – after having drummed myself into a state of excitement at the thought that I might be achieving a breakthrough into the paranormal. This, simply, to stimulate adrenalin.

After six weeks he handed me his notes and I compared them with mine. The number of coincidences, if you wish to regard them as such, were not impressive – eight out of a total of thirty, but what surprised me was that on five other occasions I had unconsciously become the receiver, for I also noted my immediate and secondary thoughts (marked †)

		Self	John
	1	Palm tree	His mother
	2	Christmas tree	His car
	3	Alsatian dog	The seaside
*	4	Red Setter dog	A dog
	5	Fox terrier dog	Flowers
†	6	Film title: 'China Syndrome'	'China Syndrome' (which he saw the night before)
*	7	Wasp	Bee
	8	Four poster bed	His house
	9	Marylin Monroe	Toy shop
*	10	Palm tree	A tree, not palm
	11	Alsatian dog	Empty theatre
†	12	Alarm clock	Alarm clock
	13	Red rose	Fields
	14	Red rose	Van Gogh portrait
	15	Red rose	Burning candle
	16	Red rose	His parents
*	17	Red rose	Roses
	18	Red rose	The Union Jack
	19	Red rose	Teapot

†	20	A nun in white	A nun in black
	21	Daffodil	His bicycle when a boy
	22	Pink tulip	Penguins
*	23	Blue plastic bucket	Blue bucket
*	24	Blue plastic bucket	Grey bucket in a sink
*	25	Tennis racket	A game of tennis
	26	Jockey in red and yellow	Ironmonger's shop front
	27	Citroen. CX Satin grey	Father Christmas
†	28	Local post office	Pillar box
	29	Empire State Building	A horse
	30	A black cat	Father Christmas again

It is interesting to note that days 23, 24, 25 were those during which he suffered a cold and had taken aspirin during the day. Was he, therefore, more relaxed?

Telepathic messages, it seems, are received as soon as they are sent, the time lapse between the thought occurring in one person's mind and it being received by the other person amounting to fractions of seconds, as far as it has been possible to gauge.

The most basic laboratory telepathy experiments are carried out with Zenner cards, a set of five clearly illustrated symbols, black on white, representing a square, a circle, a cross, a star and wavy lines. The examiner chooses one of the cards which the examinee cannot see, and the examinee has to guess which symbol has been chosen.

In the majority of cases the 'choice' score is on average 5 out of 25 attempts, but there have been some exceptional results.

Dr Joseph Rhine (1895-1980), the American psychologist and Professor of Psychology at Duke University, once heard that a nine-year-old girl from an unhappy home had scored 23 out of 25 correct answers during a school Zenner card experiment.

He had her brought into the laboratory and, making her feel important and eventually emotionally attached to one of his assistants, she managed a score of 25 out of 25.

On another occasion he challenged one of his more devoted students to attempt an exceptionally good result in a vital test, and the student identified every single playing card out of a whole pack.

Under demanding pressure from someone they wanted to please, from whom they wanted a pat on the back and compliments, in a further series of tests, it became clear that such emotion influenced the results beneficially.

Though most of his research over a long period has provided statistical evidence that only an average of eight out of twenty-five of his tests succeed, this low score is so persistent that it seems to prove that telepathy can be mastered under the right circumstances. First, therefore, create the right circumstances.

The most formidable telepathy experiment ever carried out was in 1966 in Russia, and is known as The Grand Moscow-Siberia Telepathy Test.

On April 19 of that year, a Moscow journalist, Karl Nikolaiev, travelled to the scientific academy at Novosibirsk, in Siberia, in order to receive telepathic messages from a biophysicist, Yuri Kamensky in Moscow 1,860 miles away, locked alone in an insulated chamber.

According to a report in a notable book on parapsychology studies, *Psychic Discoveries Behind the Iron Curtain*, Kamensky had no idea what type of messages he was going to send to Nikolaiev, only that he would be handed several objects on which to concentrate and that his supervisors would hand them to him one at a time and allow him ten minutes for each 'transmission'.

'The first package they gave me,' Kamensky later explained, 'contained a metal spring of seven tight spirals. I picked it up. I moved my fingers over the coils. I let both the feeling and the sight of it sink into me. At the same time, I envisioned the face of Nikolaiev. I imagined he was sitting in front of me. Then I shifted perspective and tried to see the spring as if I were looking over his shoulder. Finally I tried to see through his eyes.'

In Novosibirsk, Nikolaiev fingered the air as though for something visible only to himself. He wrote 'round, metallic. . . gleaming. . .indented. . .looks like a coil.'

When Kamensky concentrated on a screwdriver with a black plastic handle, Nikolaiev recorded, 'Long and thin. . .metal. . . plastic. . .black plastic. . .'

Nikolaiev was then later tested with another 'transmitter', giving in poorer results, though when this sender concentrated on a dumbbell Nikolaiev wrote 'metal, round, long, fat, hard, not chromed, iron bar, grey, like unpolished iron, heavy. What is it? Can it be dumbbells?'

In a test with Zenner cards chosen in Moscow, Nikolaiev identified twelve out of twenty.

This spectacular experiment, though not convincing the sceptics, compelled a large number of scientists to agree that all people probably possess telepathic powers in various degrees, that some were more talented than others, but that everyone could train that possible talent.

A GIFTED TELEPATHIST

One of the most gifted telepathists to make use of his capabilities in other ways than just experimenting was a Pole named Wolf Grigorevich Messing. He was well travelled, had met and had carried out successful extrasensory perception tests with no less than Einstein, Freud and even Gandhi, and had fled to Russia during the German invasion of his country in the Second World War – the Nazis were apparently interested in his psychic powers.

He had to earn his daily bread by giving theatrical demonstrations of his gifts, reading people's minds – performances which he considered clownish but were all the same essential to keep alive in a foreign country, and one night, in the town of Gomel, his act was rudely interrupted by two Soviet agents who arrested him and drove him off in a waiting car.

Not told what he was being accused of, he eventually found himself in Moscow, in the Kremlin, and in the presence of Joseph Stalin himself. The Soviet leader had heard of Messing's act, was fascinated by the infinite possibilities of useful deception such a person as Messing could perpetrate, and he requested him to demonstrate a number of outrageous feats.

First, Stalin asked him to rob a bank by virtually hypnotizing the bank clerk into giving him a vast quantity of cash over the counter.

Messing did this successfully, watched by police officers, returning the money to the clerk once he had proved his capabilities. The clerk, in this instance, collapsed from a heart attack afterwards, an attack which did not prove fatal.

Next the Soviet leader had Messing locked up in a Kremlin room under guard and he was told to get out without a pass, if he could. He did.

Stalin then suggested that Messing should attempt to enter his own private country house at Kuntsevo, uninvited and without security clearance, a seemingly impossible task as the house was ever swarming with bodyguards and army personnel.

But Messing accomplished it by using telepathy, managing to convince those who stopped him that he was Laventi Pavlovich Beria, Stalin's own Chief of the secret police, though he looked nothing like the man and did not even attempt to disguise himself.

Messing, from then on, was employed by the Ministry of Culture and presumably used his undoubted talents to good effect under KGB patronage, for he became a very rich man. His many experiments were regularly reported in the Soviet magazine *Science and Religion* and Nobel prize winning chemist Dr Nikolai Semyonov, Vice President of the Academy of Science in the USSR stated that, 'It is very important to scientifically study the psychic phenomenon of sensitives like Wolf Messing.'

Messing wrote about his own powers in his autobiography *I am a Telepathist*, explaining:

> People's thoughts come to me as pictures. I usually see visual images of a specific action or place. There is nothing supernatural, nothing mysterious about the ability to read thoughts. Telepathy is simply a matter of harnessing natural laws. I first put myself into a certain state

of relaxation, in which I experience a gathering of feeling and strength. Then it is easy to achieve telepathy. I can pick up on just about any thought. If I touch the sender, it helps me sort out the thought being sent from the general noise. But contact is not a necessity to me.

When I am blindfolded telepathy is even easier for me. If I don't see the sender, I'm able to concentrate totally on perceiving his thought. How clearly the thought comes through depends on the ability of the sender to concentrate. If a crowd of conflicting thoughts stream through the sender's mind, the thought-reader's impression will blur – just as the picture used to blur when someone moved in an old-fashioned time photograph. Curiously, the thoughts of the deaf and dumb are the easiest to get, possibly because they think much more visually than the rest of us. But it is time that science took telepathy away from mysticism and found out how it works. Because it *does* work! Some years ago nothing was known about radio waves. Why can't telepathy bring us similar miracles? It surprises me that scientists do not realize, or do not want to realize, that telepathy happens all the time in their own lives. Isn't this like the savants of the middle ages, afraid to waver from the doctrines of Aristotle, refusing to admit that electricity existed though they saw lightning all the time?

Russian scientists, however, are not refusing to admit that telepathy has possibilities, for they are now experimenting with a telepathy space communication system. Dr Ippolit Kogan, Director of the Popov Bio Information Bureau, has been reported in the Soviet press as saying that '. . .telepathy will have application whenever it's impossible to use other means of transmission. It can be used in space flight. Imagine the breakdown of a radio on a cosmic flight. It would be enough to telepathically transmit the number 5, for instance. This would inform earth stations that the radio was not functioning and that they should take action. Of course this would require a specialized person. He would be recruited from the gifted and properly trained. Lost or endangered expeditions on earth could also use telepathic SOS.'

Are the Russian cosmonauts using telepathy in space? In 1963, Dr Eugene B. Konneci, then Director of Biotechnology and Human Research and Technology for the National Aeronautics and Space Administration, told delegates at the Fourteenth International Astronautic Federation in Paris, 'The nature and essence of certain phenomena of electromagnetic communication between living organisms is reportedly being pursued with top priority under the Soviet manned space programme.'

PRACTISING TELEPATHY

Attempting to discover whether you have the capabilities of harnessing telepathic powers depends entirely on your determination to do so, but, unfortunately, also on one other person's equal determination for you to succeed.

So, first, catch your reliable partner who is willing to act as your devoted aide, always remembering that he may prove more talented than you, which should not in any way be seen as a set back but very much as an important plus.

The principal objects of a telepathy experiment are:

a   For the Transmitter to lock onto a 'message', preferably an 'image'.
b   Imbibe that image into the subconscious.
c   Send the image subconsciously to the Receiver's subconscience.
d   For the Receiver to receive it subconsciously.
e   For the Receiver to convey it to his conscious mind.

Stages c and d are, therefore, out of your control and it is these stages that are to be practised ad infinitum with great patience until some degree of success is achieved.

Failure is invariably due to boredom, therefore experiments should be carried out in small doses between long intervals.

Both people involved should be eager to get back to the tests, and after the first moment of 'rapport' it is obviously excitingly easier.

Five minute trials are suggested between thirty minute breaks, or longer, the intervals being spent doing something completely different. A couple decorating a flat or house create a very favourable atmosphere, both united as they are working physically on the same mentally undemanding project.

Experimental conditions are important.

There must be no possibility of outside distractions during the tests and both Transmitter and Receiver should be seated comfortably; loose clothing is advisable, as ill fitting or tight garments can cause lack of concentration. The room should be dark, neither too warm nor too cold.

The Transmitter should be in charge; check that the Receiver is ready, then home in on whatever object he has chosen, which should be handled, caressed, felt all over for about 30 seconds.

He should then wait for another 30 seconds and quietly ask the Receiver what has come into his mind.

This can be repeated about five times and then the long break should be taken.

Though Transmitter and Receiver can eventually swop over, it is advisable to stick to the same roles for at least fifty experiments, and then not make a change without several days of non experimentation between.

You are training your subconscious mind to transmit or receive, and it will confuse it, and you, if you make changes, as much as it would confuse a learner driver to drive first a left-hand drive car, then a right-hand drive car.

When success has been achieved and a good percentage of 'hits' is scored, do not move onto the next stage too quickly, but hold that success and consolidate it with practice.

Once you feel that you are mastering your telepathic abilities, then concentrate on developing yourself further.

The six stages of development should be:

1   Handled household objects.
2   Simple, single visuals. (Infant teaching books are excellent for this.)

3   Single written words.
4   Short written sentences. (The cat sat on the mat.)
5   Imagined images. (The Receiver's house, car, street, something known to both of you.)
6   A message.

Approach your subconscious as you would approach a child's mind. In telepathy it *is* a child's mind, totally under-developed.

Once Stage 6 has been successfully achieved, then distance should be put between Transmitter and Receiver, at first in different neighbouring rooms, then in different parts of the flat or house, then any distance you may wish to try.

If you have been developing well and constantly, you should check on whether you are transmitting or receiving messages from other people who may not be aware of your capabilities. This now enters into the realms of mind reading and mesmerism and you should be aware that some people may consider this to be a gross invasion of privacy. So tread cautiously.

Checking immediately by telephone that you are receiving telepathic messages is one good way of finding out how independent you have become, and if you can enter a room and instantly gauge what some people are thinking, then you can consider yourself to be telepathically minded.

But then, of course, perhaps you always have been.

3
MIND OVER MATTER

The action of mind over matter without the apparent use of any physical force became front page news in 1973 when the Israeli, Uri Geller, bent spoons double by stroking them lightly, deflected compass needles by staring at them and altered time itself when holding watches in the palms of his hands – all on television for millions to see.

Psychokinesis or telekinesis is the oldest paranormal activity recorded by unexplained historical evidence. Massive monuments, for example erected by semi-civilised tribes have baffled the most sophisticated engineers, who admit that the method of construction cannot be satisfactorily explained and that, perhaps, unknown forces were used to literally move mountains.

Mountains and monuments are not being moved today. The human mind has long forgotten how to make use of such psychic powers, but occasionally a person can stare at an object and will it to move and, far more often, subconsciously perpetrate the frightening phenomenon of levitation which marks the difference between psychokinesis and telekinesis: the former is *direct action of mind over material objects*; the latter, *the spontaneous movement of independent objects without an apparent energy source.*

Telekinesis, like any other paranormal phenomenon, tends not to be taken too seriously by scientists, but when an outstanding disturbance of poltergeist activity is reported, science quickly explains it away as telekinesis.

It is the minor of two unexplainables.

Poltergeists (from the German words *Polter* (rattling) and Geist (ghost). . .rattling ghosts) supposedly manifest themselves by loud noises and knockings, the shaking of furniture and tapping on window panes. Such unsettling commotions usually occur when a child at the age of puberty is present and can escalate to daily turmoil, the breaking of plates, of objects, the movement of large pieces of furniture, the opening and slamming of doors, or anything else that can truly unnerve. Poltergeist activity can last up to a month after which it may cease for ever, but not always.

One of the most famous instances of poltergeist hauntings is recorded in *Histoire du Merveilleux*, published in 1840, and written by the researcher into the paranormal Guillaume Figuire.

A fourteen-year-old French girl, Angelique Cottin, was at the centre of unprecedented manifestations which, in the nineteenth century, caused a great deal of alarm and speculation as to the existence of ghosts though, clearly, this was a case of uncontrolled telekinesis.

One day Angelique, the daughter of humble French peasants, was going about her business in the small family cottage on a large estate when the furniture around her started to move.

These movements escalated over the next few days, frightening the occupants of the cottage. When a heavy chest in the corner of the kitchen used for storing corn was seen to rise several feet in the air before dropping down with a crash, everyone fled in panic.

The local seigneur, who owned the land and the cottages farmed by the family, happened to be an intelligent and educated man who became fascinated by these strange activities, not believing for one moment that the furniture movements were

42

caused by phantoms, but deciding that the explanation must be scientific. Angelique, for some reason, had developed electric charges which caused objects around her to move.

Together with other friends who were either medically or scientifically orientated, he tested Angelique and, once satisfied that his theories were probably correct, took her to Paris to be examined by members of the Academy of Sciences.

A Doctor Tanchou took the case in hand and recorded that when in her presence he personally felt strange vibrations emanating from her, uncategorized forces which she could in no way have put out by trickery. On one occasion when sitting next to her on a sofa, the heavy piece of furniture was pushed rudely across the room to bump against the opposite wall.

The activity around her was so incredible and unexplainable that he consulted other scientists, including the leading French physicists, Francois Arago, a respected rationalist.

Tests carried out in his presence recorded that furniture and objects retreated from Angelique as she approached them, and chairs were playfully taken away from under her when she tried to sit on them.

As word of her extraordinary powers spread and interest grew in Angelique as a phenomenon, the Academy prepared to carry out a series of rigidly controlled examinations, but, just as the activity had started without warning, it ceased without warning, giving rise to the speculation that the whole business had been trumped up by Tanchou and Arago.

Guillaume Figuire points out in his book that 'preconceived disbelievers' and respected notables, such as those members of the Academy who claimed to have seen the manifestations for themselves would never have done so for any unscientific reason, nor indeed for any form of benefit.

Several twentieth-century accounts of poltergeist activity confirm the views of those who believe that telekinetic manifestations are usually connected with the young.

In 1958 in the middle American town of Seaford, a house in

which two children, James and Lucille Hermann, aged twelve and thirteen, became the centre of frighteningly destructive forces.

As though in a whirlwind of unseen ghostly hands, objects, cutlery, china, ornaments were hurled against walls, but the invisible power concentrated, for some extraordinary reason, on bottles. Whenever there were bottles in the house, the caps or corks were pulled off and the contents spilled.

The first and obvious explanation was of course that the liquids in the bottles, which varied, were being subjected to some form of fermentation which caused the explosions, but no rationally scientific reason could be found for this to happen.

The children's mother, a devout person, filled the bottles with holy water at one stage, but this made no difference, and the activity got to the point when the President of the Psychical Research Foundation at the University of Virginia, J.G. Pratt, and the Head of the Psychical Research Foundation at Durham, North Carolina, W.G. Roll, came to investigate the fearful manifestation.

They were in the house when a bottle of starch stored in a box in the basement popped its screw cap, spilling its contents all over the floor. The cap was found some distance away and no evidence of any gasses having caused the activity were found.

On another occasion bottles popped in the bathroom and other toiletries were moved around.

An aunt, staying with the children one afternoon, saw a figurine lift off a table in one corner of the room and hover to the centre carpet where it dropped to the floor without breaking. While this happened she was able to watch James Hermann who apparently sat unconcerned on the sofa with his arms folded.

Because of this incident, James became the focus of the researchers' attentions and it was discovered that the further the objects were from the boy, the weaker the poltergeistic activities. It was concluded that such a telekinetic energy was governed by the same laws as those which govern other forms of energy, i.e. the nearer the source of energy, the stronger the manifestation.

Another well known and more recent example of a child causing telekinetic activity was recorded in 1960 in a remote Scottish village. An eleven year old girl, Virginia Campbell, was not only the centre of poltergeist manifestation in her home but the energy forces followed her to school – a very rare occurrence. In the classroom her teacher observed the phenomenon of a terrified Virginia desperately trying to keep the lid of her desk down but finding it impossible to do so. The lid opened and closed slowly of its own accord with an incredible strength, and then the desk was shifted several feet out of line.

On another occasion while Virginia stood by the teacher's table with her hands behind her back, the stick which the teacher used as a blackboard pointer rose from the table to drop a few feet away.

Psychokinesis is, I believe, the most difficult paranormal force to try and train. It is more of a gift than a latent power, but every attempt should be made to find out if the 'other you' is hiding it.

URI GELLER'S GIFT

Uri Geller plays an important part in my writing career, for it was his radio broadcast in 1973 preceding his famous television appearance, which started me off on the quest for my other self, albeit, at that time, to convert any experience to entertaining fiction.

This BBC radio broadcast took place on the Jimmy Young show one November morning and I will quote Uri Geller's opening passage from his autobiography *My Story* for he can best explain what happened and how he felt:

> When I went into the tiny BBC radio studio to be interviewed by Jimmy Young, I wasn't prepared for what was going to happen. I was ready for something, but nothing as big and as mind blowing as what followed. . .Jimmy began with the usual questions. He asked when I had first found out that I was able to bend keys, nails or other metal

objects just by touching them lightly and when I had learned I could start up a watch or clock that hadn't run for years. I said I had noticed these things way back in my first years at school, much to the surprise of my classmates, my teachers, my parents – and also myself. In fact, I am still surprised, and I still have a sense of wonder when these things happen.

Then he asked me if I would demonstrate for him. Of course I had agreed to try before I went on the show. Jimmy took a thick Yale key from his pocket and put it down in front of me. I did what I usually do, laying my hand over the key and wishing it to bend. Jimmy was watching carefully, and by this time the engineers in the control room were peeping through their window. Everybody was expectant and excited. I continued to be a little nervous myself, because sometimes these demonstrations do not work, which is very embarrassing for me. I am confident that they will work most of the time, but there is still that chance that they won't.

What usually took place during Geller's psychokinesis demonstrations was that he either rubbed a key or a nail between forefinger and thumb and it started to bend. Or sometimes he simply held his hand over the metal object and it would start to bend, continuing to bend after he took his hand away. The objects had been known to bend up to 45 degrees or even a 90 degree angle, sometimes the metal melted without apparent heat, and half the key dropped off.

Some months before, in Texas, Geller had done a similar radio interview. A few days later he had received a signed affidavit from three officials of the Texas Attorney General's Office who had listened to the broadcast and, for their amusement, had put a number of metal objects on the table in front of the radio. The handle of a spoon had bent 45 degrees, a door key had completely broken in half, and a large paper clip had vanished into thin air. What had been astounding however, even to Geller himself, was that they had been listening to the demonstration when Geller was no longer there, for the show had been taped and broadcast hours after he had left the State of Texas.

In the BBC studio, while still rubbing the key, with Jimmy Young telling the listeners what was happening, Geller said into the microphone, 'If there are any broken watches in your house, please concentrate on them and try to make them work. Just take them in your hand and concentrate on them.'

The key was bending and Geller wondered what might be happening beyond the studio, for the show was being broadcast in England, Wales, Scotland and Ireland.

Jimmy Young then became excited, startled by what was happening before his very eyes. 'It's bending right in front of me,' he shouted, 'I can't believe it!'

Continuing the story in Geller's own words:

> The studio producer then rushed in with a bunch of notes. I didn't know at first what they were all about, so I kept talking. I explained how I was always as baffled as anyone else when I bent a key or a spoon.
>
> The producer continued running in and out of the studio with one note after another. Then I realized what was happening. The entire BBC switchboard had lit up like a Christmas tree. There were phone calls from England, from Ireland, from Scotland, from all over the British Isles. All England seemed to be bending. The phone calls were reporting that knives, spoons, keys, and nails were bending in homes everywhere, near and far from London. A lady from Harrow reported that she was stirring soup when suddenly the ladle started bending. The gold bracelet of a girl from Surrey buckled and bent. A police constable said that several knives and spoons had curled up. A jeweller reported that half the pieces on a tray of cutlery bent. A watchmaker said that his tweezers had done the same. There were reports of watches and clocks starting up that hadn't run for years.

The next day Uri Geller was national news, such headlines as 'Uri Puts Britain in a Twist' and 'Uri Catches Britain Bending' screamed out from the front pages, and he was invited to appear that night on the David Dimbleby television Talk In, together with Dr Lyall Watson, the biologist and author of Supernature, and Professor John Taylor from the department of Mathematics at King's College, London University, who were to supervise another psychokinetic demonstration.

> Various things were spread out on a table: forks, spoons, broken watches, and keys. I suggested that the audience concentrate while I

was concentrating. Dimbleby held a spoon in his hand, and I stroked it lightly with two fingers. It bent almost double in a very short time. As the spoon was bending in Dimbleby's hand, a fork on the table bent without anyone touching it. I stroked another fork, and it bent until the handle broke off and dropped on the table. Then I began concentrating on the broken watches on the table. They began starting up almost immediately. Lyall Watson's watch, which had been running perfectly, suddenly stopped. The hands inside one of the other watches suddenly curled up against the crystal.

Professor Taylor who had begun the programme with a sceptical attitude, seemed to be shocked by what was happening. So did the others. The demonstration couldn't have been more successful. And any doubts I'd had about the effects of the television show throughout England were cleared up immediately. The BBC switchboard was jammed, so jammed that it was almost put out of commission. The same thing had again happened in homes everywhere. Even on the Channel Island of Guernsey, three families had seen their spoons bend and broken clocks start up.

Before leaving London, Geller agreed to another experiment suggested by the newspaper *Sunday People* which had a circulation of fifteen million. The idea was that at a specified time Geller, wherever he was, would shout 'Bend!' and that all readers interested in joining in would hold various metal objects and concentrate on bending them.

At Orly Airport in Paris on Sunday 25 November at 12.30 p.m., Geller concentrated his thoughts on things metallic in a northerly direction, then continued on his way to an appointment.

The *Sunday People* received more than a thousand letters, during the week that followed, claiming that hundreds of broken clocks and watches had started up of their own accord and that forks and spoons had bent all over Britain.

The paper published the results in its next issue:

Clocks and watches restarted	1,031
Forks and spoons bent or broken	293
Other objects bent or broken	51
Total:	1,375

Dr Edward Bastin, a mathematician at Cambridge University, stated in the newspaper, 'The question that now needs to be asked is whether the owners influenced the objects themselves, or whether Uri did so through them.'

NELYA MIKHAILOVA

As scientifically incredible as Uri Geller for her psychokinetic powers, but a good deal less famous because she lives in Russia, is a Leningrad housewife Nelya Mikhailova, who has spent years being tested by Soviet physicists.

Holding her extended fingers six inches above a compass on a table, then moving both hands in a circular motion, she has made the compass needle spin in the same direction as her hands and often, after twenty minutes of hard concentration, moved the compass itself, its plastic case and its leather strap, causing all to glide clockwise or anti-clockwise on the table surface.

Faced with a number of different objects she has also proved herself selective. By staring at a pile of matches she has made them move individually to the edge of the table and drop off one by one.

One day, at home with a grandchild in her arms who wanted a toy on the other side of the room, she caused the toy to come towards her. On another occasion, when her nails were wet with varnish she managed to screw on the cap of the polish bottle by will power.

Mikhailova believes psychokinesis is inherited. Her mother had such powers and so has her son. It is a family gift which they use to their own advantage, often for amusement. The Soviet writer Vadim Marin, who worked with the Popov Research Group described an incident: 'Mrs Mikhailova was sitting at a dinner table. A piece of bread lay on the table some distance from her; Mikhailova, concentrating, looked at it attentively. A minute passed, then another. . .and the piece of bread began to move. It moved by jerks. Towards the edge of the table, it moved more smoothly and rapidly. Mikhailova bent her head down, opened her mouth, and, just as in the fairytale, the bread itself jumped into her mouth!'

In an extraordinary laboratory test, her power over foodstuffs was studied at length: the most outstanding result was when she managed to separate the white from the yolk of a raw egg immersed in a glass tank of brine, then put the two substances together again, upsetting the credible theory that psychokinesis only worked with metal objects due to some form of electromagnetism.

In 1935, Dr Harold Burr, Professor of Neuroanatomy at Yale University, put forward the idea that all living matter from plant seeds to human beings was enveloped by an electrodynamic field which ensured that new tissue grew to the proper size. Dr Leonard Ravitz, a Neuropsychiatrist at the same university later proposed that this force field could be influenced by the mind.

Fifty years later Dr Genady Sergeyev, working at the A.A. Uktomski Physiological Institute in Leningrad started work on this theory, inventing a machine that could detect the electrostatic and magnetic biological fields from about four metres distance from the body without any form of contact. Tests carried out on Mikhailova revealed that her brain generated fifty times more voltage readings from the back of her head than from the front, and with other tests he concluded that vibrations in the fields around her body acted like waves, causing objects on which she concentrated, whether magnetic or not, to behave as though they were magnetized – as scientific an explanation of psychokinesis as anyone can wish to get.

Further to this, however, the Sergeyev detector was set up a few metres from a clinically dead man, with unnerving results. Though no heartbeat or brain activity could be recorded, energy from electromagnetic force fields was released.

Mind over matter, then, is probably mind-over-force-field-over-matter, an idea which is backed by another Russian discovery that psychokinetic tests proved more successful when magnetic disturbances on the earth caused by sunspot activity were recorded.

In a Soviet paper, scientists have declared that they believe three things contribute to the ability to generate psychokinetic power:

a   Human emotion, both from the active person and those surrounding them.
b   Natural magnetic forces produced by the sun, the moon, or earth movements.
c   Force fields produced artificially by machine.

Most important, for any personal tests you may wish to carry out, is the belief that negative influences from other people are very disruptive to successful results. If you seek help from friends or relatives, therefore, *they* must believe in what you are doing, and be one hundred per cent behind your efforts.

The sceptical sneer is very destructive to the possible psychic who *must* be regarded, indeed nursed, as an ultra sensitive person, especially in the early stages of trying to discover what powers lie undetected within him.

NINE EXPERIMENTS TO DISCOVER PSYCHOKINETIC POTENTIAL
Spend at least half an hour on each.

1   Sit in a totally dark room and concentrate on a battery operated torch switched on in front of you. Make the greatest effort possible to cause the light to blink or waver. Try this with a tired battery to begin with, for energy is minimal and you are trying to register microscopic force field impulses. Simple electrical appliances can lead to discovering powers within yourself. Bear in mind, however, that a tired battery tends to waver of its own accord. Judge whether *you* are affecting it by studying it after a flicker when you are not fully concentrating.

2   Concentrate on a battery-driven clock which has stopped. Will it, with all your might, to start up again *or* try to stop a working clock. Clocks with second hands are obviously essential for this experiment.

3   Switch on a transistor, find a clear musical programme (talk distracts attention) and concentrate on the transistor itself in order to cause static interference. Should you get a crackling sound when you look at the transistor then you should work hard on yourself for this is a clear indication of high potential. The transistor is acting as a geiger counter to your powers.

4   Switch on a television programme which does not distract you too much – a programme of no interest to you personally. Concentrate on causing the picture or the sound to waver. Even if you get the very slightest reaction, consider this a major step. But you must repeat this success several times before shouting victory. Outside interference must always be taken into account.

5   On a smooth, flat surface sprinkle a line of fine sand or salt, about six centimetres long and one millimetre wide. Concentrate on the centre of this line with the grim determination to dent the line.

6   Hold a thin piece of metal – a cheap tea spoon will do – between forefinger and thumb, rub it gently, concentrating on having the metal bend by your will power.

7   Mercury is not readily available except in thermometers, so go mad and break a thermometer in order to get a drop of mercury which should be contained in the plastic lid of any household container. A plate will not do as they are rarely flat. Concentrate on moving the mercury bubble just a fraction. If you split it, then consider yourself extremely potent.

8   Place a ping-pong ball in the centre of a table. Make sure there are no draughts. Concentrate on urging the ball to roll towards you or away from you. If you succeed, will it to move in whatever direction you choose.

9   Place a number of household objects of different materials on a table before you, concentrate on one object at a time for about

five minutes, then move on to the next, willing the object to move. One, or several objects may react though they may not have your full attention. If so, experiment in moving objects of those materials which react most easily to you.

Try: matchsticks, pins and needles, glass marbles, pebbles, green leaves, dry leaves, flower petals, strands of animal and human hair, small pieces of cotton wool, dried fish bones, droplets of water, tiny pieces of paper, cut up pieces of magnetic tape, tiny pieces of broken glass, plastic buttons, etc. . .

4
PSYCHOMETRY

The (alleged) faculty of divining, from physical contact or proximity only, the qualities or properties of an object, or of persons or things that have been in contact with it.

1845. J.R. Buchanan. 'The influence of psychometry will be highly valuable in the selection of candidates for appointments to important offices.

1863. Denton. 'Mrs Denton, by means of this science of Psychometry, professes to be able, by putting a piece of matter to her forehead, to see, either with her eyes closed or open, all that piece of matter, figuratively speaking, ever saw, heard, or experienced.

The Oxford English Dictionary

The sceptic word 'alleged' in brackets in the Oxford English Dictionary meaning of *psychometry* is yet another indication of how difficult it is for anyone who suspects that they may have psychic powers to talk about it openly without fear of ridicule. To be paranormal, it seems, is tantamount to being a witch and to practise psychometry no doubt equivalent to dabbling in sorcery.

Minority groups have always been persecuted; just remember

that this particular minority group might eventually prove to be very much a force to be reckoned with.

The J.R. Buchanan quoted in the Oxford Dictionary was Professor James Rhodes Buchanan, Dean of the Faculty at the Eclectic Medical Institute in Covington, Kentucky, who invented the word 'psychometry', based on conclusions, deduced from various experiments, that some people had the ability to discover information relating to an object by the sense of touch alone.

A certain Bishop Leonidas Polk, he found, was able to recognize brass from other metals in the dark because it gave him a particularly acid taste in the mouth, and a number of tests carried out on his students revealed that many could detect different kinds of medicines and liquids, although these were contained in a bottle which was wrapped in paper and sealed. He believed that our nerves produce a certain type of vibration in the form of taste, smell or colour – a 'nerve aura' – when the psychic subject touches an object, and that this information given by the nerve aura, correctly interpreted, can be very detailed.

William Denton, a friend of Buchanan and Professor of Geology, experimented with archaeological findings and, in a book entitled *Nature's Secrets* described how a psychometrist holding a piece of lava from a Hawaiian island was able to describe 'an ocean of fire pouring over a precipice' and how a glacial limestone pebble produced sensations of being frozen into ice and deep under the sea.

According to Colin Wilson's *Mysteries*, Denton was convinced that the whole history of the earth is imprinted in the objects that surround us and can be read by anyone who takes the trouble to develop the faculty. He concluded that one man in ten, and one woman in four, is able to read the past in this manner.

Psychometry, or object reading, shares an unfortunate fuddy-duddy reputation with clairvoyance – represented by Noel Coward's Madame Arkarti in his play *Blithe Spirit*.

This image is typified in this 1844 letter from the *Medical Times* quoted in the *Encyclopedia of the Unexplained* about Alexis

Didier the mid-nineteenth century clairvoyant who demonstrated his power of object reading in a London house.

> Colonel Llewellyn, who was, I believe, rather sceptical, produced a morocco case, something like a surgical instrument case. Alexis took it, placed it to his stomach and said 'The object is a hard substance, not white, enclosed in something more white than itself; it is a bone taken from a greater body; a human bone – yours. It has been separated, and cut so as to leave a flat side.' Alexis opened the case, took out a piece of bone wrapped in silver paper, and said 'The bullet struck here; it was an extraordinary ball, in effect; you received three separate injuries at the same moment; the bone was broken in three pieces; you were wounded early in the day whilst engaged in charging the enemy.' He also described the dress of the soldiers, and was right in all particulars. This excited the astonishment of all the bystanders, especially the gallant Colonel. This account is drawn up, not only from my own notes, but from Colonel Llewellyn's statement after the seance, and from a written account given me by a lady who was sitting close by.

Bringing psychometry history more up to date, in 1912 Rudolph Tischner, a German ophthalmologist, tested a woman who claimed to have telepathic powers. These powers proved in fact to be psychometric for when he took a postcard from a large box in which he kept all his past correspondence, sealed it in an envelope and handed it to her, she wrote down, after holding it for a few minutes, five out of the twelve words that were on the card and described the picture – a house with trees – correctly.

Suspecting that he might have glanced at the card unwittingly when handing it to her, remembered its message and communicated it to the woman by telepathy, however unconsciously, he asked a friend to pick out another card from the box, double wrap it and seal it in an envelope and hand it to the woman, while he was in another room. Observed, the woman held the package for a few minutes, then wrote down everything that was on the card and described the picture correctly.

Though these tests were not earth shattering, they are a very good example of the simplest form of psychometry which many people find they can develop in themselves.

Ten years later, in England, the first 'psychometric detective' made her appearance in a very amateur way, but all the same heralding the acceptance of this supernatural power by the most doubting of groups in our society – the police.

In April 1922, Eric Tombe, a young ex-army officer disappeared without trace.

His parents moved to the house in Surrey where he had lived and naturally searched through all his belongings in the hope of finding an explanation. At about this time his mother, perhaps not unnaturally, started to have nightmares that her son was dead, but always with the same recurring theme, that he was buried in a well which was sealed by a massive stone slab. These dreams troubled her enormously for they became more and more vivid and few people were disposed to be sympathetic. To say that she felt her son was 'entombed' gave sceptic friends and doctors an excuse to write off her visions as 'name association' but her husband, the Rev. Gordon Tombe, took her seriously and eventually convinced the police that a search for a well around the house should be carried out.

They found no wells, but four cesspits, all of them sealed with massive stone slabs. One of them was found to contain rubble, and when this was removed they discovered the body of Eric Tombe who had been shot in the head at close range.

A murder enquiry followed and eventually the killer was brought to justice.

Though one explanation put forward was that Eric Tombe had contacted his mother by telepathy from the well before dying, the autopsy disproved this theory as Tombe had died instantly from the bullet that had shattered his skull. That Mrs Tombe might also have received guilty telepathic messages from her son's murderer, is a possibility, but the explanation that was accepted at the time was that she had simply gathered psychometric information while sorting out her son's belongings and imagined she was having nightmares when in fact she was receiving clear messages from the objects she was handling.

This true account of course must make us realize that we are entering the realms of the unexplainable.

That a person should be able to read the message written on an antique postcard, or read history in a human bone, is one thing, but that they should receive directions as to where a body lies hidden from clothes or objects that that person handled *before* he died, hints at the unrealistic. How can objects record a future tragedy and have that tragedy visualized after the event?

THE PSYCHIC PETER HURKOS

The incredible story of Pieter van der Hurk must now be recounted, for this man with undeniable supernatural powers is the living evidence that we are all capable of developing psychically – either by accident (as in his case) or by working hard on ourselves.

In The Hague, July 1941, the Dutch people were trying to lead normal lives under the German occupation, but some businesses were failing, among them the professional house painter Van der Hurk who had reluctantly had to take on a contract for the painting of a tall city building from the Germans in order to survive.

His son Pieter, thirty years old, an amateur by his father's standards, had to help, and while the elder van der Hurk coped with the intricacies on an indoor ceiling, Pieter painted the less noticeable window casings outside on the fourth storey.

To save time and energy he set up his ladder precariously between two windows so that by stretching he could first paint one, then the other without going through the dreadful business of moving all his equipment.

But the obvious tragedy happened.

'I can never forget this,' he recalls in Norma Lee Browning's biography, *The Psychic World of Pieter Hurkos*. 'I hang over, and then I slip over and the ladder falls. And that moment I was falling, I saw my whole life pass before me, and I didn't want to die. I want to live. I was fighting, fighting, from the moment I was falling down from the ladder, because I didn't want to die. And then I fall down and everything was black, and I remember when I tried to get up because I want to live, I want to live! But then it was black, for a long time black. I was in darkness.'

Concussed for four days he miraculously survived the precipitous fall because, according to witnesses, he landed on his shoulders,. On awakening he thought he had only been asleep for five minutes.

'Everything was so beautiful, the flowers, the mountains, the music. Like people singing far away. And when I come out conscious, there was no colour. It was all dirty, grey, one colour, and I couldn't stand the light, it was like a knife in my head.'

He had, in fact, lost his memory for most things, finding it hard to recognize faces, but knowing who his friends and relatives were by the sound of their voices. When his wife, Bea, first came to visit him she believed he had gone insane. She had left their baby son Benny with a neighbour, and Pieter had suddenly sat up in bed and screamed out, 'Bea, what are you doing here? Where's Benny? You belong at home with Benny. You shouldn't be here in the hospital. You're not a good mother. You go now and get Benny. Quick! Now! Oh God! The whole room is burning with Benny!!'

Benny was in no danger whatsoever, on that particular day, but a week later their home was engulfed by fire and the child was only just rescued in time by firemen.

Shortly after this strange and upsetting incident, Pieter surprised a nurse by suddenly grabbing one of her arms.

'Be careful when you go home on the train tonight, or you will lose your valise.'

The nurse was astounded by the prophecy – for it had already happened, the night before, and there was no way he could have known.

Some days later another patient from the hospital, who was being released, came to say goodbye and when they shook hands

Pieter held on tightly, not wanting to let go. Once the man had diplomatically managed to get away, however, Pieter blurted out to a nurse that he feared for the man's life. He had sensed he was a British secret agent and that he would shortly be shot.

Two days later the man, a spy working for the British secret service was shot, and the repercussions of this vision nearly caused Pieter's own death, for the German authorities heard of his prediction, would not believe his claims to being newly psychic, and decided to eliminate him.

In the hospital, two men visited Pieter van der Hurk. They questioned him, then quite suddenly pinned him down and held a pillow over his face to suffocate him. Pieter struggled, managed to shout, and what he shouted saved his life.

'How I hate killing!' he screamed out. 'How I hate killing!'

They were the thoughts of one of the men, who then became convinced that Pieter had not been lying about his powers.

Before he was released from the hospital a few weeks later, Pieter had an embarrassing brush with one of the doctors. While he realized that most of the staff thought him mad, he himself was beginning to accept that his fall had caused his brain to shift in some way and that he was now clairvoyant. It was an unpleasant and frightening feeling and he hated it.

'I thought I was crazy sometimes. My life was like a nightmare. I didn't want to see all these things, these pictures and voices. Sometimes it didn't matter if I saw a person or not. If I touched an object like the water pitcher next to my bed, I would hear sounds. When I touched the wall I would hear sounds and see things. Sometimes I would put the pillow over my head to cover my ears and eyes, but these pictures and sounds would always come to me. And even when I slept, my mind would travel to places I had never seen before.'

Begging the doctor to test him to find out if he had developed paranormal faculties, he asked to be handed an object. The doctor gave him a pencil. Rubbing it with his fingers Hurkos said, 'I see you have pyjamas with stripes that look like a tiger.'

The doctor was not impressed, pointing out that most people had striped pyjamas.

'But your pyjamas, sir, have the initials G and D in designs. GD, and the pyjamas were given by your girl-friend who is a nurse, and you have a child from her and you are still married. And your wife asked you where you got the pyjamas and you told her you bought them yourself. But the design GD was done by your girl-friend.'

All of which was true and surprised him so much that he could not believe he had these psychometric powers, to the point that he naively repeated a similarly embarrassing scene once he was out of the hospital.

Needing to know more about the world of the paranormal he attended the performance of a well-known psychic who asked individual members of the audience to write messages on a piece of paper which he would then burn before revealing what the message was. A friend of Pieter's sent up a message, the psychic burnt it, then told the audience that he had a message from a Pieter Hurkos who claimed to be more psychic than himself. And he invited Pieter up on stage.

Pieter explained that when he touched objects he got certain visions, and the psychic, amused, handed him his watch.

Pieter held it for a while, receiving a number of visions, then he declared that the watch contained a lock of blonde hair from a woman who was close to the psychic's heart, but not his wife. He further revealed that the woman's name was Greta and that she travelled everywhere with the owner of the watch, then added, 'She is in the audience now.' At this point the performer requested Pieter to go back to his seat, but on his way Pieter was drawn to a person in one of the front rows – a blonde woman. 'That's her, that's Greta,' he pointed out. And he was right.

From then on Pieter van der Hurk started working in the entertainment business, reading people's objects with successes that surprised him. Then he was called on to help police in a crime they could not solve.

A young coal miner in Limburg, South East Netherlands, had been shot. Pieter asked to be given articles of the victim's clothing, and the police handed him the coat he had been wearing at the time of death. Holding the coat Pieter told them that he believed the man had been killed by his step-father who was in love with his wife. They might find the murder weapon on the roof of the victim's house.

The police searched, found a pistol in one of the gutters of the dead man's house, ballistic tests proved this to be the murder weapon which, together with finger prints led to the arrest and conviction of the victim's step-father.

On another occasion, in Rotterdam, Pieter was asked if he could confirm the death of a man who had fallen over the side of a ship docked in the harbour. Handed a piece of the man's clothing, Pieter very quickly stated that the person was indeed drowned, then, when he visited the port, immediately pointed to an area of the oil slicked harbour water, suggesting that a search should be carried out there.

A few hours later the body of the drowned man was found by divers in forty feet of water at the exact spot, entangled in weeds and garbage.

Pieter van der Hurk first became known in England when he paid a visit to London in order to solve what was considered at the time as a fearful crime against the Royal Family and the State, but was in fact all a bit of a lark.

Someone, in 1950, stole the Stone of Scone, the sacred slab of granite which nestles beneath the Royal throne in Westminster Abbey.

The Stone was somehow kidnapped from the Abbey in December of that year, a few months before Elizabeth II's coronation, and naturally caused great concern to the powers that be. A number of psychics, clairvoyants, telepathists and even water diviners saw in this escapade a great opportunity to prove their abilities, among them van der Hurk who, no doubt, needed as much publicity as any other entertainer.

After visiting Westminster Abbey and touching the throne to sense vibrations, he told the authorities that five people had been involved in the abduction, three of them had entered the Abbey while two had remained outside. The plot to steal the Stone had been hatched in conversations near the Round Pond in Kensington Gardens, the culprits were students from Scotland and the Stone was more than likely now in Glasgow. The whole thing, as far as he was concerned, was no more than a student's prank.

The authorities did not see this so much as a prank as a major slight on English history and Royal tradition, thanked van der Hurk for his help and left it at that.

On returning to Holland Pieter found himself held up for three hours by customs officials who clearly had him labelled as a suspect – he just knew too much for his own good. In time, however, his theories were proved right. Scottish students had taken the Stone, five had been involved, the crime had been planned in Kensington and the Stone had travelled to Glasgow.

In 1958 van der Hurk went to live in America, changing his name to the simpler Peter Hurkos. He settled for a while in Miami and there was called on by the police to help them solve a murder.

A cab driver had been shot in his taxi, there were no clues, nothing whatsoever to go on, except a .22 calibre pistol.

Hurkos asked if he could sit in the driver's seat and, after a short while, had visions of a tall thin man who walked like a sailor. The man, he sensed, had a tattoo on his right arm, definitely came from Detroit and was called 'Smitty' by his friends. He had killed before, quite recently, in Key West while ransacking a house.

Police enquiries were put under way, a naval officer was found to have been shot in Key West by the same pistol that had killed the Miami cab driver, and the Detroit police identified 'Smitty' as Charles Smith, a wanted member of a crime syndicate.

Hurkos worked with the police on many other cases, some more successful than others, then made world headlines when he joined the detection team involved in the notorious Boston Strangler murders.

Between 1962 and 1964 thirteen women were raped and strangled in the Boston area. Financed by an industrialist who believed in his psychometric powers, Hurkos presented himself to the local police who were not at all keen to have him on their team, totally doubting his psychic detection abilities.

He pulled out all stops, however, by first rejecting a trick photograph they gave him of a supposed victim – telling them that it was a plant to catch him out, then delivering a below-the-belt salvo by contradicting a police officer who turned up late for a meeting with the excuse that his car had broken down. 'That's a lie,' Hurkos corrected him in front of his superiors, 'You are late because you have just visited your girl friend and had sex.'

After this he accurately described what had happened to each of the victims whose photographs were set before him, though they were placed on the table face down.

Hurkos's involvement with the Boston Strangler case is reported in great detail in his biography, suffice it to say that he states categorically that the Strangler was a man who was mentally ill, a homosexual woman hater who washed his hands in his victims' blood, all of which information he claimed to get from one of the letters the police handed him, written by a character who invited nurses to partake in photographic modelling.

Information gained through so-called psychic powers is not admissible as legal evidence. The police could not find other proof that Hurkos's man was guilty, and eventually they arrested and accused another, Albert DeSolvo, a schizophrenic who was committed to a mental asylum. Hurkos has always maintained that the police accused the wrong man.

In 1968, while Hurkos was appearing as a cabaret turn in Palm Springs, he was approached by the Police Department and asked to locate a missing aircraft.

A flying instructor Robert Cline, with co-pilot Frank Carpenter, had lost radio contact with San Diego while on a flight from Phoenix. For two days a wide area had been searched but no trace of the plane had been found.

Hurkos, as always, asked for some of Cline's or Carpenter's belongings and after holding some of their clothes for a long time – according to his biography – declared, 'Both dead. I'm sorry. I hope I'm wrong. But that's what I see. He changed course in a storm. . .Nine miles off course. . .I see two dead. The engine was overhauled not long ago. . .The trouble is not with the engine but with the tail. There is too much pressure on the tail.'

Spreading a large map of the area (upside down so that he would not be influenced by names and figures) Hurkos then took out a pencil and started tracing lines on it.

'This is where they started, and this is where they got off course. . .in these mountains. He planned that course exactly, he is a good pilot, but when the storm comes he changes course. The plane is not in a lake, but I see water, like a creek or a stream. The plane is near a stream, under trees and bushes, hard to find. . . here.'

And he marked the map with an 'X'.

The plane was in fact found six miles east of where he had pin pointed its position, and three bodies were found, not two. Aboard, Cline had had a student, but the oddity of Hurkos's vision was that Cline and Carpenter were found outside the crashed aircraft, under trees and not far from a stream, while the student was found trapped inside the buckled fuselage.

The psychometry practised by Peter Hurkos, like that of Mrs Tombe, can best be categorized as 'clairvoyant psychometry' – a mixture of seeing and sensing the past, the present and the future, examples of which are not at all rare.

In a book *Exploring the Ultra Perceptive Faculty* by Dr J. Hettinger, who carried out hundreds of experiments to prove the reality of psychometry, he records his many results. His tests were simple; he sent psychometrists various articles or letters belonging to other people through the post and they wrote back stating the visions and sensations they experienced when coming into contact with them. An object from a school teacher created a vision of school desks in a row; an impression of someone drowning was received from a letter written by a man who had later drowned. What was curious, and clearly 'clairvoyant psychometry', was when Hettinger received a result describing a fire and the person whose object had created this vision suffered in a fire *after* the test had been recorded. This could be called 'precognitive psychometry'.

Historic psychometry, when the visions are only of things past, is easier to understand, if you accept the theory that all objects retain the vibrations of what they have experienced.

In the 1930s one of the first 'historic psychometrists' to gain world renown was Stefan Ossowiecki, who lived in Poland.

When handed a package containing an unknown object, he declared without hesitation that it was extremely old, several thousands of years BC, human – a petrified foot.

It was in fact a mummy's foot, and he later added that it was an Egyptian girl's foot, the daughter of a high ranking official who had died at childbirth – an interesting case history which of course could not be verified.

In 1973 another psychometrist, George McMullen, was asked to demonstrate his powers at a banquet given by the Canadian Archaeological Association in Toronto. McMullen was handed a crudely carved black stone head of a negro. After a short while he stated that it had been carved by a negro, from Port au Prince in the Caribbean, who had been brought to Canada against his will as a slave.

The archaeologists present were disappointed as they knew the head to have been found on an Indian site off British Columbia on the Queen Charlotte islands. Later McMullen was given another chance to 'read' the head, stuck to his story adding that the slave was West African and had been taken to the Caribbean to begin with before he was bought by the English who shipped him to Canada. There he escaped to find refuge among the natives of an Indian tribe near British Columbia where he spent the rest of his life.

This whole case history was checked by the archeologists and eventually found to be absolutely correct.

One of the most recent and rather outstanding examples of psychometric detection occurred in 1980 when Suzanne Padfield, a well known psychometrist and clairvoyant from Somerset, was sent a photograph and schoolwork of a Russian girl called Innesa Tchurina. In December 1979 the nine-year-old girl had gone skating in Fryazino, outside Moscow, and had never returned. All attempts to find her had failed.

Suzanne Padfield received the Innesa items through the post via a psychic friend, but had no idea that they were going to be sent to her nor who they belonged to.

She opened the parcel on receiving it and on handling the objects had instant sharp visions of a young girl in a skating rink talking to a heavily set man with a beard. She saw both leaving the rink together and walking down an unfamiliar street, the man tempting the girl to come to his house to look at a new pair of skates. The visions developed like a film: once home the man, attracted to the girl, became very nervous, unsure of what he wanted to do with her, and the girl, picking up these vibrations, became very frightened, tried to get out and started to scream. Not wishing her harm, the man, Suzanne Padfield felt, panicked stupidly and hit her on the head. The girl collapsed, and the man, becoming totally paranoid, strangled her.

Suzanne Padfield saw him wrap the girl up in a large blue garment, hoisting her on his shoulders, leaving the house and getting onto a bus. He went to a river and dropped the bundle in, after which the vision ended.

The psychometrist sensed that the man was in his thirties, had a round face, but now wore no beard. He had run away from his home and was no longer in Moscow.

All this information was sent to the Russian police who, unlike Western authorities, tend to take the readings of psychics more seriously. Suzanne Padfield's man fitted the description of a suspect they had on their files, and when they eventually caught up with him and read him out a description of what he had done he confessed immediately, astonished that the police had apparently found so many witnesses.

In his statement he declared that he had wrapped Innesa in a blue blanket and had managed to get onto a commuter train without anyone taking much notice.

My own brush with psychometry is indirect, but all the same interesting. I was writing one of my psychic thriller novels *Ouija* in which a female character had to discover that she was clair-voyant, and I decided to base this extraordinary episode in her life on a true story. A Greek lady I knew, who lived in Paris, actually recounted the following which I put down nearly word for word in my book.

> She had not considered the idea (of being psychic) seriously until she had held a private sale in the apartment for friends and aquaintances, and one of them had been interested in a little brass box that looked very old because of its faded velvet lining.
> She had told the woman that it had once belonged to Napoleon's manservant because when she held it in her hand she got visions of battlefields, and the woman had been very impressed and had said that she must have psychometric powers.
> 'Of course I have. I can tell you the history of all my objects,' she'd boasted, and the woman had immediately handed her an earring. 'Can you tell me about this, then?' She had made up some fanciful story about it belonging to the Empress Eugenie because it reminded her of one worn in a portrait by Winterhalter. The woman had been astonished.
> 'I lost the other, could you tell me where it is?'
> 'You lost it when?' she had asked.
> 'Many years ago, we were staying with friends in Touraine, in a château, it was such beautiful countryside.'
> She had closed her eyes, demanded silence from everyone, then had pronounced that the woman had lost it while on a picnic.
> 'I was on a picnic!'
> 'You lost it in a long meadow, with tall grasses, I can see the place quite clearly, but it is built over now, large farm buildings.'
> The woman had believed her, had gone away happy and had paid a ridiculously high price for the little brass box, and everyone had said she had an obvious future as a clairvoyant with such a rare gift. . .

It had all been pretence with guess work, a château in beautiful countryside had suggested picnics fairly obviously, but she had seen the new farm buildings and had had a very strange sensation of actually being there.

In the novel, the female character is frightened by the possibility of being psychic, whereas in real life my Greek friend tested herself again and again with other people's belongings, accurately guessing their history. Then, one day while shopping in Safeways in High Street Kensington, near where she was staying on a visit to London, a stranger handed her a silver Dunhill cigarette lighter believing she had just dropped it.

'I don't smoke,' she replied. 'It's not mine. It belongs to an Italian gentleman staying at the Penta Hotel in Cromwell Road.'

'Then you can give it back to him,' the man said, smiling, and disappeared.

My Greek friend realized she had no idea why she had spun out this story of the Italian at the Penta Hotel, it was complete fabrication. She realized that the man had taken it for granted that she knew the Italian, that the Italian had lent it to her, and she became intrigued by her own story and, with time on her hands, went to the Penta Hotel (now the Forum) and made enquiries at the reception desk about any foreign gentleman who might have lost a silver lighter.

Now – was this coincidence? A Greek gentleman visiting London for the first time from the village of Meligala in the Peloponnese, where my friend herself had lived as a child, had lost the lighter and had left a note at the reception desk.

The two Greeks met and found much of their past in common and my friend later explained that she had said he was an Italian because she had instinctively known the lighter belonged to a Greek but, being Greek herself, had feared that the man who had handed it to her might become suspicious. Like many people being handed a 'lost' item of value, the thought of keeping it had crossed her mind as instantly as her psychometric detection.

Perceptions, impressions, intuitions, instinct and sensitiveness are all the things you must release from yourself with total open-mindedness when first setting out to discover if you have psychometric capabilities.

The selection of objects to 'read' is important for some articles give off better vibrations than others.

Articles connected with one person only are advisable, new jewellery rather than old – necklaces which are worn close to the skin transmit the owner's personal history more clearly than a brooch on a dress.

Keys are bad for they tend to be handled by a number of people, like coins which should always be avoided.

Small items of clothes are less effective than large; hats and scarves are often worn by several people or left on public tables and stands.

Gloves tend to be very personal because of size and these should be turned inside out to get the personal magnetism more strongly.

Shoes, though also very personal, naturally tend to pick up everything around, so are quite unreliable. Items of underwear invariably prove the most rewarding, but are not the easiest things to ask for, for obvious reasons.

Letters have a great deal to offer. However, the person they have been written by and the person they have been written to have to be separated. Double readings can be confusing.

The selection of persons from whom you borrow articles is also very important, for if you know them well you subconsciously read something you already know. So interested and, again, even sceptical persons are best. Their surprise at a successful reading will be genuine.

EXPERIMENTING IN PSYCHOMETRY

For your first experiment in psychometry you should get someone to give you a necklace or bracelet or wrist watch belonging to a person you do not know.

When you are in a relaxed state you should concentrate on the object you are holding for a minute or so then deliberately 'let go' allowing the mind to wander in order to let images and impressions come in on you.

Such images are so simple that they may be difficult to recognize. You may get a violent impression, something quite surprising and unusual, the picture of a person with an extraordinary expression, or something frightening like the development of a fearful accident, but usually it will be a fairly serene scene, a home, a garden, someone riding a horse, or a bicycle in a country lane perhaps, who can tell? This picture, whatever it is, has to be translated into meaningful terms, held on to and made to work.

The person helping you should be close by to assist you in this by just listening. You can use a tape machine. What is important is the feeling that someone or the tape running, waiting to record is there, anxious to hear what you have to say. This urgency forces you literally to speak your mind, and you can then go over what you have said afterwards, analyse it and assess its value.

Apart from images you may receive sensations. You may even feel pain. Do not ignore this, note it down, record it. If the person to whom the object belongs has not yet suffered such discomfort, maybe they will.

Initially, keeping a record of all your psychometric thoughts is essential, for if you are a clairvoyant psychometrist, it is only noting down your thoughts of one day that will enable you to check up on their precognitive substance when/if they become reality several months later.

The paranormal has no perception of time.

One cannot stress enough that an enormous amount of patience is needed, specially to begin with. A psychometrist getting impressions may depend on his or her health, phases of the moon, the weather, what they have eaten, how the adrenalin is flowing or not flowing. Psychics, it cannot be emphasised enough, are sensitive persons – which means they may be sensitive to any-thing – and only by keeping a detailed record of successes *and* failures, and under what circumstances the experiments took place, can a complete pattern of capabilities emerge.

To illustrate how a perfectly normal person discovered that she was a psychometrist, I print below the correspondence which both of us exchanged over a certain period of time.

I received a letter one day from Australia from a lady who had read one of my books. Some of its action took place in Melbourne where she lived and I let the letters themselves tell the rest of the story.

Melbourne. 15th June.

Dear Mr Laurance,

I have just read your trilogy *Premonitions of an Inherited Mind/The Link/The Embryo*, all of which I much enjoyed. But you have never been to Australia have you?

I did not deduce this from your writing, you cleverly sidestep all possible pitfall descriptions, but for some time I have found that I truly 'read between the lines' – that is get impressions from people's letters and newspaper articles about the people who write them.

From your book I have got this:

You have green eyes, a fair complexion, you are in your thirties and worry a great deal about manufactured problems when you do not have genuine ones, you are irritated by dogs – there is a dog barking somewhere in your life – you sometimes live by the sea but suffer from dizzy spells and feel unhappy on water.

Please write to me and tell me if I am right, and if so what I should do to improve this gift.

Yours sincerely
Angela Macdonald

London. July 2nd.

Dear Angela Macdonald,

I have brown eyes, a dark complexion. Score zero.

I am middle aged. Score two for flattery.

I am inwardly anxious, yes. Score 10.

Until I received your letter I was unaware of the barking dog as important. However, next door, there is such a dog who does irritate me a great deal. Score 50.

72

I live some of the year in a seaside village in Spain. I occasionally have bouts of imbalance due to suffering from labyrinthitis a few years ago, I am therefore easily seasick. Score 100.

You are clearly a psychometrist.

(I then suggested and discussed what has preceded in this chapter and ended. . .)

I therefore enclose a postcard received from Portugal recently, and will confirm, or not, whatever impressions you send me.

Best wishes,
Andrew Laurance

Melbourne. 19th July.

Dear Andrew,

The Portuguese Postcard

I got a very faint impression of an elderly lady with a straw hat and roses. An aunt, perhaps, travelling abroad? Nothing else.

Best wishes,
Angela

London. 15th August.

Dear Angela,

The Portuguese postcard was sent to me by a 40-year-old male friend searching for a holiday home in that country.

I can think of no connection between him and roses or an old lady in a straw hat. But I will check.

I enclose a leather bookmark.

All the best,
Andrew

(The leather bookmark was dark green with *Westminster Hospital* embossed on it in gold.)

Melbourne, 13th September.

Dear Andrew,

The Bookmark

I naturally immediately got an impression of someone lying sick in bed – tried hard to discard this, together with images of nurses and doctors with stethoscopes. Too easy.

73

Aware that I was being influenced by 'Westminster Hospital' I put it down for two days and took it up again when in a state of near sleep last night.

This time I got a very clear picture of a woman in a wheelchair without legs and a terrible feeling of worry, but not from her. Just from someone else, possibly you. I would deduce from this that you have recently been visiting someone in hospital who has suffered a major accident.

Yours, etc. . .
Angela

London. 1st October.

Dear Angela,

The Bookmark

Quite remarkable.

The bookmark was given to my wife when in the maternity ward. (She recently gave birth to a little girl.)

After visiting her one day I got into the crowded hospital lift. Into the crowded lift a nurse pushed a woman in a wheelchair.

One of the wheels accidentally went over my foot and the nurse apologized profusely.

Jokingly I said, 'It doesn't matter. I have another anyway.'

Only then did I realize that the woman in the wheelchair had no legs.

Needless to say I was extremely embarrassed (worried?) and to this day still react with a spine chill to my awful 'faux pas'.

In my hand I was holding the bookmark.

I enclose a comb.

Yours, etc. . .
Andrew

Melbourne. 19th November.

Dear Andrew,

The Comb

Nothing. Quite honestly nothing at all. I have tried several times, but get what I would term a totally negative reading. I have had 'flu and am still rather weak. Maybe that is why.

Yours, etc. . .
Angela

Over the Christmas period I sent her a greetings card.

74

Dear Andrew,
    Was the Christmas card a test piece?
    When I opened it I got an instant and very clear picture of an elderly person, male or female I could not tell, sitting in an armchair wearing a wine coloured dressing gown with a zip right down the middle.
    Could it be Father Christmas?

                              Yours, etc. . .
                                    Angela

                              London. 14th January.

Dear Angela,
    The Father Christmas was possibly my grandmother, who lives in France. She always wears a red dressing gown of your description. I had just written a letter and card to her before I signed the one to you.
    Meanwhile, my friend who went to Portugal (Postcard experiment) came to dinner last week. His wife gave him a magnificent book on roses for Christmas because it is his new hobby. He acquired an interest in the flowers when in Portugal visiting his English aunt, 'Who lives like a typical English country lady in a rose covered cottage.'
    I enclose a piece of silk material.

                              Yours, etc. . .
                                    Andrew

The experiments and exchange of letters continued for a while longer, without any major surprises, rather more failures, then, due to pressure of work and Angela Macdonald moving house, we gradually ceased to correspond regularly.

    I then received this last letter:

                              Melbourne. 7th October.

Dear Andrew,
    A month or so ago a very dear friend of mine handed me her husband's wristwatch asking me to give her a reading. As I knew he was ill, I was very concerned and cautious and pleased to get a clear image not of anything horrible like a sick bed or a funeral (which I feared). Instead I got a picture of a bright green car.

She thanked me and said little.

Yesterday, not having heard from her for a couple of weeks, I tried to contact her and learned that she had gone to Adelaide to stay with her parents following an attempted suicide. Her husband left her after she had found out he had been having an affair with his secretary. She found out because he had given his girl-friend a green car for her birthday! The person who told me all this added 'You should really be a bit more careful Angela, dabbling with your black magic. They used to burn people like you in the middle ages.' You will understand, therefore, why I have decided to give up my psychometry.

Yours, etc. . .
Angela

I answered her stating that I very much regretted her decision and, dramatically, quoted Horace:

You are dealing with a work full of dangerous hazard, and you are venturing upon fires overlaid with treacherous ashes.

To this I added: 'nothing risked, nothing gained. . .'

5
PHOTOKINESIS

Thought-o-graphy, images produced on photographic plates or film by the mind.

Only three names have become famous in connection with this astounding paranormal gift: William Hope, Ted Serios and, again, Uri Geller.

Coupled with the first two, Tomokichi Fukurai and Jule Eisenbud must be given prominence for their undoubted patience in this field of phenomenal work.

Photokinesis is such a rare supernatural talent that anyone who discovers it in themselves should scream the news from the rooftops as they have a duty to society to let it be known, simply because it would be proof of what humans can do.

I have to admit that I know of no one personally who can claim to be a photokinetic, though a friend of mine saw Uri Geller demonstrate what he could do with a camera.

Between 1910 and 1913, Tomokichi Fukurai, then Professor of Physics at the Imperial University of Tokyo, carried out a series of experiments testing a psychic who seemed to be able to register mind images onto photographic plates.

The psychic thought of a picture, stared into the lens of a camera and that picture – not the psychic's eyes – was reproduced on the photographic plate when developed.

It was such an unbelievable idea that Fukurai was unable to convince his fellow professors that the work he was doing was genuine and, labelled a charlatan – though they had no proof whatsoever of skullduggery – he was forced to resign his position.

In the 1920s he came to England and heard of a spiritualist named William Hope, who had been accused of fraudulent activities. He realized that the man was in the same boat as himself and started his experiments again to prove them both innocent.

Hope, after a very short time, managed to produce thought images on Fukurai's photographic plates, and though he believed that the pictures he created came from the world beyond, pictures of people who had died, pictures of scenes sent to him through the dead, Fukurai was certain that they had nothing whatsoever to do with spiritualism but were thought transferences of a quite incredible but down to earth kind, a force which turned imagination into reality with the help of photographic chemicals.

Unfortunately, due to their reputations, Fukurai's experiments were never taken seriously enough and eventually proved so expensive that, like countless other unsuccessful pioneers in the paranormal sciences, he had to give up and disappeared without trace.

TED SERIOS – THOUGHTOGRAPHER

In 1964 virtually fifty years later, Fukurai's name was revived when the world sat up to take notice of a phenomenal man who claimed and proved that he could take photographs with his brain.

Ted Serios from Chicago was exactly the type of person researchers in the supernatural do not need. Aged 45, an ex-hotel porter, unemployed and an alcoholic by reputation, he had been the subject of an article in the American *Fate Magazine*, written by Pauline Oehler, Vice President of the Illinois Society of Psychic Research.

A series of tests carried out with Ted Serios had proved that he could project photographic images onto Polaroid film by staring with great concentration into the camera lens.

The article claimed that his psychic photography had produced pictures of the Pentagon, the dome of the White House, the entrance to the Chicago Museum of National History, the gardens of the Taj Mahal and a number of street scenes, all quite recognizable, though slightly out of focus.

The article further claimed that the tests carried out over a number of months had been verified by scientists, photographers and other 'intelligent observers' and that no fraud had been possible and, to underline this, Mr Stanford Caldewood, Vice President of the Polaroid Corporation, stated in a letter to the President of the Illinois Society of Psychic Research:

> Let me stress that while a clever man could tamper in advance with our film, I know of no way he could do it if you were to show up with the film you bought in a store at random and watched him load and shoot. Tampering with the film would be a long and complicated procedure and nothing that could be done by sleight-of-hand, especially if he had to photograph two or three pictures (or thoughts) on the same roll without reloading the camera and without an opportunity to substitute something in front of or behind the lens.

The article and Ted Serios' claim to fame might have been forgotten there and then if, during the year that followed, Dr Jule Eisenbud, Clinical Professor of Psychology at the University of Colorado, and Fellow of the American Psychiatric Association, as well as a member of the American Society of Psychical Research, had not published a paper on the supernatural, arguing that experiments in psychic phenomena could be made to happen once, but seldom twice, which meant that 'the repeatable experiment in parapsychology would take its place alongside the alchemist's stone and the cabalist's tetragrammaton, with those dreams of mankind which would remain forever dreams . . . '

This article caused parapsychologists to react angrily. They wrote to him by the dozen and among the objecting letters that he received there was one enclosing the cutting from *Fate Magazine* about Ted Serios as proof that repeatable parapsychological experiments were possible.

Dr Eisenbud moved fast. He met up with Ted Serios as soon as it could be arranged and put him through a whole series of tests, all of which were so successful that he published a very full and detailed volume on the project entitled *The World of Ted Serios – Thoughtographic Studies of an Extraordinary Mind*. In it he explains his work method:

> I began by withdrawing a fresh film pack from its sealed container and loading the Polaroid Land type 100 camera that I had brought and which I hadn't up to that time allowed out of my sight for a moment. I hadn't had too much experience investigating sensitives or alleged mediums, but I knew just enough, chiefly from a fair acquaintance with the literature on this type of research, to realize that some of the cleverest deceptions had been achieved right before the eyes of observers who imagined that, because of conventional training in one or another scientific discipline, their methods of observation and control were infallible . . .

Serios was helpful at all times and not in the least bit secretive. If Dr Eisenbud wanted to hold his hands or examine them he made no objections. He said he had a preference for a Polaroid camera Model 95, but the Model 100 to be used would do, this was only because he did not like the brightness of the flash attachment of the latter.

The following account of the experiment carried out was noted by an assistant, additional notes being made by Dr Eisenbud a day or so later.

> At 8.50 Ted indicated that he was about ready to go. He predicted that he would get a long tall structure with a sign 'crosswise' on it. He then removed the coins, the keys, and a rosary from his pants pocket and

laid them on a nearby table top, explaining that he felt that the presence of metal on him interfered with picture taking. More small talk. Ted smoking away. Finally Ted indicated that he would like to try to fog the first film without touching the camera or tripping the shutter. Would we mind if he took his shoes off?

At Ted's request I held the camera about two feet from his head pointing at it. The shutter was left uncocked. Ted sat in a chair, leaning forward toward the camera. He said he would try for a small dot and a large dot. He concentrated for a couple of minutes, complained of a headache, and said that was it, that he had finished, that he had tried for a plus sign. (He then told us that concentration was very difficult, that he sometimes bled from the mouth and anus immediately afterwards, never at other times.)

Print No.1, the first try, came out perfectly black on development.

At 9.32. Ted was ready for his second try, this time holding the camera and tripping the shutter himself. For this he fished out of his pocket a device which we later came to refer to as the 'gismo'.
(Note: The gismo is important, for it was a home-made device, a short plastic funnel-like tube which Serios placed over the aperture fanning outward so that any light or shadows which might hamper the image he concentrated into the camera were kept to a minimum. Though the gismo was said by some to be a device which helped Serios pull off his trick thoughtography, it was examined by too many sceptical academic colleagues of Eisenbud's for this to be possible, besides which Serios was often capable of producing well defined pictures on double wrapped unexposed film. Sometimes Serios in fact produced photographs when blindfold and more often than not when the camera had no lens. His power was that of mind over photographic film.)

When about to shoot, Ted seemed rapidly to go into a state of intense concentration, with eyes open, lips compressed, and a quite noticeable tension of his muscular system. His limbs would tend to shake somewhat, as if with a slight palsy, and the foot of his crossed leg would sometimes start to jerk up and down a bit convulsively. His face would become suffused and blotchy, the veins standing out on his forehead, his eyes visibly bloodshot.

On trial No.2. Ted asked to be given his target envelope. For this I had used a heavy-grade manila, with cardboard covering the image side. Ted held the envelope in front of him for a few seconds and said, as he handed it to me, 'It's an entrance, a driveway entrance or walkway.' (It was a color photograph of part of the Kremlin that I had taken the summer before). I tried not to let my facial expression indicate that he had missed – an almost impossible task, of course – and held the target envelope for him next to the camera, as he

81

requested. As he got set for the shot, his breathing became deeper and faster until the flash came. When the print came out – completely dark again. Ted still showed no sign of loss of composure but merely changed his guess as to the photo hidden in the opaque envelope. 'A group of buildings with two people,' he suggested, but without even a trace of the question mark in the voice that is so characteristic of some psychics fishing for clues. He asked, however, for a short rest.

After another three tests resulting in black positives, they tried for the sixth:

At 11.04 Ted took shot number 6. This print showed some unusual, rather amorphous, fogging and one or two lines or shadows that I didn't stop to examine at the time but which Ted thought showed beginnings of activity. Because his heart was pounding away at a fast clip now, a fact which he demanded I verify by feeling through his shirt, he asked for the camera again immediately and took the next shot at 11.05. A blackie. Ted demanded the camera again immediately and shot number 7. When developed it was at once apparent that we had something here that was a picture of a recognizable structure.

Mrs Morris (another assistant who came in to watch) excitedly identified it as the Chicago Water Tower and started to jump up and down, clapping her hands. Young Jon, who set about to fix the print, said nothing, as if this were the sort of thing that he saw every day of the week, while I, less excited about the crude mechanical oddity of what had just occurred than about an interesting peculiarity of the picture that would have meaning to no one but me, started to expound on what had struck me so forcefully and its relation to the phenomenology of telepathic dreams seen in analysis.

At 11.40, (after a rest) Ted started to stir. He had a hunch that on his next picture he would get something that would be meaningful to both Jon and me. He got set to shoot and went through his normal procedure.

His eleventh picture of this set of experiments came out as, what Eisenbud terms, 'a bull's eye'.

Glowing in the centre of a murky but nonetheless quite distinguishable 'photograph' were the letters STEVENS on an illuminated sign over the marquee of the old, no-longer-standing Chicago Hotel (it had burned down some years before.)

Ted identified the Stevens as the present Hilton and thought that it had not been known under the name Stevens for the past thirty years. He had no particular memories connected with it and couldn't imagine why it should turn up. And, contrary to Ted's prediction, it carried no special meaning for Jon or me as a structure. The *name* STEVENS, however, did ring a peculiar bell.

The peculiar bell which rang in Dr Eisenbud's mind was that the last colleague he had spoken to about the experiments he intended carrying out in Chicago with Ted Serios, was a Dr James Stephens, Head of the Department of Neurology at the University of Colorado. Dr Stephens was a biting critic of Eisenbud's beliefs and it could be presumed that subconsciously Dr Eisenbud had Dr Stephens lurking around in his mind during the thoughtographic tests. However, as Eisenbud himself explains:

I had always been firmly of the opinion that the unconscious, with its wide ranging abilities and limitless facilities, does not make for simple errors like mistaking *Stephens* for *Stevens*, and that if *Stephens* had actually been intended *Stephens* it would have been, as Ted's unconscious could easily have found a graphically expressed plot into which to weave it, even if an illuminated sign bearing it were not conveniently reposing in the files of his memory. Thus I remained rather ambivalent toward this possible interpretation of the Stevens Hotel picture and, after my first flush of interest on seeing it turn up so soon after my discussion with Jim Stephens and his attitude toward psychic phenomena, would probably have thrown it out had it not been for the fact of what it seemed to accomplish as a magical pick-me-up for my ego. But some time later I happened to learn that Ted's unconscious was no better at spelling than his conscious mind and could be demonstrated to have made mistakes even less excusable, from the schoolmaster's point of view, than misspelling a name that I daresay many of its possessor's friends might misspell in exactly the same way.

Dr Eisenbud received a picture taken by Ted Serios of a building that looked like a warehouse, somewhat out of focus, but with distinguishable letters that appeared to be something like AIR DIVISION CANADIAN MOUN. The building was eventually identified as that belonging to the Royal Canadian Mounted Police, an Air Division hanger, but on the picture itself, on close inspection, the word Canadian was actually misspelt 'Cainadain', proving undoubtedly, it seems, that Serios's thought photographs were exactly that – photographs from his thoughts.

In Dr Eisenbud's book, one hundred or so of Ted Serios's

photokinetic pictures are reproduced, some of which are really quite incredible.

But though exceptional, Ted Serios is not the only thought-ographer alive. Uri Geller, when visiting England in 1970 proved that his psychic abilities could also affect unexposed film. During a photographic session with the press, he upset a number of professional photographers by taking pictures of himself by facing a camera which had a cap over the lens.

The passport type photographs of Geller produced by this unexplainable method appear in his autobiography (*My Story*) and the story has it that the *News of the World*, annoyed that another Sunday paper should get this exclusive of Geller's self portraits, sent their own photographer Roy Stockdil, an ex-tremely experienced man, to see the psychic. He loaded his camera, screwed the lens cap tightly on the lens and clipped it down and watched as Geller photographed himself.

Developing the film himself afterwards, he found that most of the negatives were black, but that several were clear pictures of Geller which were good enough to be used in the next issue of the paper.

In order to find out whether you have thoughtographic poten-tials, it seems that you have simply got to hold a camera at arm's length facing you, concentrate into the lens, think of a particular image and click the shutter.

If you get a blurred picture of yourself, this is not surprising. But if you get a photograph of anything else that could not remotely be anything to do with your surroundings, then exper-iment until you produce images which you know you have forced onto the negative by sheer will-power.

Also cap the lens and try to photograph yourself.

I have tried both these methods, with abysmal results. I am not a bit surprised, but then I try everything that might lead to an indication of paranormal activity within the other me.

6
CLAIRAUDIENCE

Clairaudience is the clear hearing of sounds and voices which others cannot hear, through superphysical perception and/or the subconscious. The words clairaudience, clairsentience and clairvoyance all originate from the French followers of Dr Anton Mesmer (1734–1815) who was able to convince people that he had total control over them by practising the art of what was then known as Animal Magnetism, later Mesmerism (after his name) then Hypnotism, a word coined by Mr James Braid in 1843.

Sceptics prefer to believe that any form of extrasensitiveness is somehow related to hypnotism. I believe that certain people are capable of, among other things, hearing sounds and voices which others cannot, because they can tune into different sound waves, as can dogs, which for some reason has been found quite acceptable.

Dogs can't talk but can hear high frequency noises. People can talk but cannot hear those frequencies. Or can they?

Tribal magicians or Shamans, dating back to the Stone Age, believed that the spirits sent them messages, as did the Gods, by the loudly spoken word, and there are countless examples of clairaudience in the Bible, not the least of which can be found in

Exodus 14:15: 'And the Lord said unto Moses, wherefore criest thou unto me? speak unto the children of Israel, that they go forward.'

In *Samuel* 1:3 . . . 'The Lord called Samuel, and he answered, Here am I. And he ran into Eli and said, Here am I, for thou callest me. And he said, I called not, lie down again, and he went and lay down. And the Lord called yet again, Samuel. And Samuel rose and went to Eli, and said, Here am I, for thou didst call me. And he answered, I called not; lie down again. Now Samuel did not yet know the Lord, neither was the word of the Lord yet revealed to him. And the Lord called Samuel yet a third time . . . '

A clear case of Samuel not wanting to believe his own clairaudic powers.

Joan of Arc could be said to have 'suffered' from clairaudience, since her voices sent her to the stake, but that she heard them loud and clear is too well documented by history for anyone to have doubts.

Angels told her she would find a sword behind the altar of the chapel of Sainte Catherine de Fierbois, which she did, they also told her when she would be wounded. She believed in her voices so much, they were so real to her, that even though she knew that talking about them in front of her judges would brand her a witch and send her to her death, she could not deny them.

Later notables in history were more cautious about publicising their clairaudient capabilities, but history books have handed down to us the fact that John Calvin (1509–1564), who systematized the Protestant doctrine and organized its ecclesiastic discipline (therefore not a man who would lie or fantasize) heard loud drumming noises when the Huguenots went into battle at Dreux and were in great danger. Because of these ominous sounds he asked his followers to kneel down and pray for all the souls he knew would be lost.

Witches stopped being burnt at the stake or executed in the eighteenth century, but after that anyone claiming to hear supernatural sounds was believed to be a bit of a looney. Certainly if you started hearing voices now and answered them in the presence of other people, they might well have doubts as to your sanity.

Clairaudience can obviously be linked with telepathy, but there is a difference. Telepathic messages are usually from live people sent to you from some distance away, whereas clairaudient messages come from the subconscious and seem to warn of forthcoming danger or tragedy – one way in which precognition in fact manifests itself.

There are many examples of modern day clairaudient warnings, the most interesting of which are detailed in Brian Inglis's *The Paranormal*. Two, connected with listening to the radio are curious, the man who heard President Roosevelt's announcement of the Japanese attack on Pearl Harbor some minutes before the announcement was actually broadcast, and the wife of a former governor of the BBC who, seven hours before the news was broadcast heard that Senator Goldwater had won the California primary against Rockefeller. Not world shattering, but examples of quite typical clairaudience.

Tito Gobbi, the opera singer, in his autobiography tells how his dead brother Bruno – killed a few months before in a plane crash – shouted 'Stop at once!' in his ear when he was driving up a mountain pass. Terrified, he stopped, just as an articulated lorry, out of control with failed brakes, came tearing down the road, avoiding a collision which would have sent Mr Gobbi over and down the precipice, a clear case of a clairaudient prediction.

Composers, of course, could be said to be clairaudient, for they obviously hear the music they are about to compose before they note it down. I think, however, that composers, like playwrights who hear and invent dialogue in their heads, are simply creative people and can only be regarded as clairaudient when the music or dialogue suggests something which they sense has nothing whatsoever to do with them.

Saint-Saëns (1835–1921) has recalled that the opening of his *Requiem* in fact came to him in a clairaudient way during the

Franco-German war. He heard the mournful music which was not at all of his own creation, it made him feel incredibly sad and anxious, and later he learned that at the time he heard it a very close friend had been killed.

Accounts of clairaudience from researches in the paranormal by scientists and historians invariably seem to be connected with death – messages of foreboding, that is, from those about to die.

Camille Flammarion (1842–1925), the French astronomer who delved not only into the sky beyond but the worlds beyond, cites the case of Linnaeus, the Swedish eighteenth-century botanist, who was woken up one night by the recognizable footsteps of his friend Karl Clark walking round his museum. It was impossible for his friend to have got into the building which was all locked up, and after investigations which proved that no one was around, he went back to bed. A few days later, however, Linnaeus heard that Karl Clark had died at the very same hour that his footsteps had been heard.

Flammarion, in his book *Des Forces Naturelles Inconnues*, also recounts the story of a girl, who for domestic and health reasons decided on a secluded life in a nunnery. When bidding her aunt goodbye, she promised the tearful old lady that if at any time she felt she might die, she would make contact and come to say adieu. Some years later the aunt and her family were terrified for several minutes when shattering noises in the house made them all believe that they were experiencing an earthquake. The aunt suddenly thought of her niece in the convent and announced that she was dead. The noises stopped immediately. The following day news of the niece's death was confirmed.

In *The Paranormal* Brian Inglis mentions clairaudient activities experienced by Sir Walter Scott in his Selkirk house which he described as 'a mysterious disturbance' in a letter. Scott and his wife were awakened at two in the morning by a violent noise like the drawing of heavy boards along the floor of the new part of the house. He thought no more about it, but the following night 'at the same witching hour, the very same noise occurred'. Scott was unaware of it but the designer and builder of the new house had died at the very same hour that the noises had been heard.

There is also the story about a Bordeaux woman who, in 1907, was woken three times by a voice calling her name, then learned later that her fiancé, who had been prevented from marrying her, died that night after calling out for her anxiously several times.

Clairaudience is the one psychic activity with which I can claim to have had some experience, not once, but three times, and fortunately only one of those times was morbid.

My first and clearest clairaudient hearing was when I was fifteen and taking my School Certificate Examination – Elementary Mathematics I. Monday, July 12, 1948. 2 hours.

I was in the great hall of the school with that uninspiring smell of pencil sharpenings, rubber and well scrubbed faces up my nostrils, an imposed silence broken only by afrighted coughs, scratching of heads and desperate sighs, and I stared with profound fear and trepidation at the exam paper before me, certain that I would not be able to answer anything because Maths was not at all my forte.

Section A, Question 1 virtually paralysed my nervous system and instantly turned my brain into damp cotton wool.

A motorist drives a car 3000 miles in one year. He uses 1 gallon of petrol costing 1/11d for every 25 miles and 1 pint of oil costing 1/– for every 300 miles. His other expenses (including licence, insurance, garage etc.) amount to £48 for the year. Find the total cost of running the car.

Now, believe it or not, a female voice, quite unrecognizable, but soft and gentle, whispered loudly over my head – not in one ear or the other – but somewhere above me, 'Sixty pounds'.

'What?' said I, out loud.

Three heads turned, the examining master was at the other end of the hall and did not hear; I panicked, really wanted to talk to someone but couldn't, finally regained control of myself and wrote down £60.

I went straight onto the second question, the third and fourth, and only when I had finished the twelfth and last question – Calculate the lengths of CN and CA giving each in inches correct to three significant figures – did I look over my answers again and have doubts as to my sanity.

The bell went before I could check answer 1, but I did as soon as possible afterwards and found it to be correct. I could not then, and I cannot now, calculate a simple multiplication problem without writing it down. Figures have always baffled me, yet I had heard the clear correct answer in a flash.

To this day I do not know whose voice I heard, or why. I only know that it gave me the confidence that I was being watched over by some sort of guardian angel and that I would therefore probably pass the whole awful exam – which in fact I did.

The second clairaudic experience was shared with two other people, my wife and a friend with whom we were dining in her London flat. There were only the three of us, we were having coffee after a good meal, we had not had much to drink, and we were enjoying a normal gossippy conversation.

Quite suddenly a male voice addressed us from the direction of the fireplace which we were all more or less facing and it said either, 'It *won't* matter in the end, it's all up to you,' or 'It *must* matter in the end, it's all up to you.'

The confusion that followed in the analysis of what had been said, to whom it had been addressed, by whom and why, together with a search for a device which some joker might have hidden, revealed absolutely nothing. Our conversation was irrelevant to the message, and vice versa, none of us could even recall having thoughts which were pertinent.

Though we expected some great revelation to follow, and kept in close contact with our friend in the hope that she would hear the voice again, nothing that could be called an answer ever came to light.

My most recent experience has to do with death and because of this I would put forward the theory that clairaudience is probably connected with the telepathic messages transformed into an auditory impulse by the receiving subconscious.

If a dying person thinks of you and subconsciously sends you a message, you may receive it subconsciously yourself, store it, and put it out as a voice or noise when you are more receptive.

The person who died was connected with Fleet Street, had been ill for some time, had been in hospital for a cancer operation and was unlikely to live for very long.

I heard his voice when I was writing something rather derogatory about him in a novel. I had based a character on him and was contemplating using a story about him he had told me which was not very honest – and I had hesitated.

I had hesitated because of conscience, I felt guilty at using a sick man's experience, especially as that experience was ultimately going to lead to his fictional death, and in actual life he was dying.

His voice, again loud and clear, and coming from somewhere over my head, said 'It's good. Use it you silly bugger.'

I subsequently heard that he had died in hospital that day.

All the examples mentioned above are accidental; they were not 'brought on' or 'willed' and though I have tried many times to hear supernatural sounds or voices around me I have never been able to. This does not surprise me because I personally believe that clairaudic sounds are one way telepathic messages sent by someone which you subconsciously receive *if* you are sufficiently developed in this particular psychic field.

My exam voice could be explained in this way, therefore. A woman exam setter who knew the answers to the paper and also knew that thousands of children were sitting down that morning studying her question in all probability answered her own question on their behalf. I, with probably many other 'sensitive' children, received that message.

When the voice talked to my wife and friend in the London flat stating that, 'It must matter in the end, it's up to you,' it could have been any man addressing someone sternly, verbally or in his mind, and all of us picked it up. The fact that three people picked up on the same message is perhaps a bit far fetched, but we may all have been lulled into a certain mood or we subconsciously plugged into an anxiety trace – more about which later.

Clairaudience and clairsentience are gifts which are within us, but they are very difficult to develop because they depend on other people sending the messages – however they very much form part of the overall ability to be clairvoyant, and this you can train yourself to become.

7
CLAIRVOYANCY

Clairsentience is the ability to feel or to sense supernatural activity. This enters into the realms of perturbed spirits and things that bump into you in the night, and before moving on to the main link to clairsentience and clairaudience, which is clairvoyancy, I would like to banish to the dusty cobwebby ghost story shelves for ever the idea that we as human beings have it in us to contact the dead.

We cannot.

What we can do is make contact with what the dead left behind, which may very well include their thoughts and projects for the future which are powerful enough to influence us.

Ghosts and spirits, phantoms and apparitions, are anxiety traces.

We are surrounded by television and radio waves continually which we cannot see or hear without the help of mechanical receivers. It is therefore just as likely that human traces, anxiety traces, left behind in places where tragedies have occurred where they are stuck in certain wave bands that we don't normally pick up on unless specially developed, exist for our examination.

Walking along a railway line where there has been a train

disaster might jar the sensitive workings of your subconscious for you to hear calls for help. Entering a room where a person died in violent circumstances might cause your subconscious eyes to see the victim – agony or fear being the strongest reactions we broadcast into the atmosphere.

The very idea of ghosts, coupled with the fear of a manifestation, can become close to a paranormal experience. If you are frightened of the dark, then you must sit alone in a darkened room until you overcome that fear by working out why you are frightened. The dark is an excellent laboratory for discovering the 'other you'.

If you are afraid of walking down a lonely lane because of violent human contact, this is too basic a fear to be dealt with in this context, but if you are frightened of ghosts, of the supernatural, of apparitions, then you must overcome this and go out and meet the very things that you think might harm you.

I have only twice felt a presence, and those never really strongly. Once in an old rectory in Dorset which was up for sale, I felt the walled garden at the back was particularly oppressive, so much so that I ran from it feeling threatened. I did not tell anyone this at the time because it sounded too obvious – an old rectory and in Dorset, the home of too many fictitious hauntings. But the other haunting was in someone's drawing room in a 1930s suburban house during a drinks party. Six of us were happily chatting away when the conversation suddenly ceased, as though interrupted by a strange sound. It lasted for a fraction of a second and none of us mentioned it immediately, but when we had got over the 'visit' we all admitted to having sensed something unpleasant, and one guest claimed he saw a black shadowy shape standing by the door. The host told us that the house had the reputation of being haunted – a death connected with an army officer during the Second World War, but up until then he had never seen or heard anything.

In a room in my London apartment I have always felt cold, even when the central heating was full on – a coldness that has nothing to do with actual temperature but with atmosphere. And I have never been able to sleep easily there. I have sat in it many times alone on purpose, daring something to come up, but apart from imagined hands grabbing my throat, or the feeling that someone was standing behind me smiling inanely, I cannot claim to having seen anything, felt anything, except the cold fingers of my own imagination.

Forcing myself to stay in that room in the dark, however, helped me overcome a fear of the unknown and taught me how to relax by allowing the mind to go blank, an essential preliminary to preparing oneself for a clairvoyant experience.

So, what is clairvoyance? Can you train yourself to become clairvoyant if you have never experienced any form of psychic sensation in your life?

In the *Oxford English Dictionary* clairvoyance is defined as:

> A supposed faculty attributed to certain persons or to persons under certain mesmeric conditions, consisting in the mental perception of objects at a distance or concealed from sight.

To this could be added, 'The faculty of seeing, without the use of the eye, events taking place at a distance at the same time or in a time warp.' For the timing of clairvoyant sightings is responsible for clairvoyance being confused with precognition – a subject which is dealt with later.

Psychometry is often mistakenly called clairvoyancy, but it is a separate psychic ability. Clairvoyance is often labelled 'second sight' or 'travelling clairvoyancy' for the person, *in his mind*, does travel short or very long distances to perceive what is happening elsewhere.

CLAIRVOYANTS EXTRAORDINARY

The most famous clairvoyant in history was the aforementioned professional theatrical performer – Alexis Didier.

The son of a man who had the reputation of falling into trances for no explainable reason, he and his brother inherited the strange faculty of seeing things happening in places where they had never been.

In the 1840s Alexis Didier was employed as a clerk by a transport firm in Paris, run by a certain Monsieur Marcillet. One evening, attending a hypnotist's performance he volunteered to be a subject. In a trance he described things which he could not possibly see with such great accuracy, that the hypnotist encouraged him to become a performer himself.

His employer, Marcillet, was then so astounded by his clerk's abilities that he backed him as a clairvoyant artist, performing the hypnotism himself.

Didier's forte was to name playing cards blindfold, never making a mistake, even putting the cards face down on the table and naming them correctly at random. He then went on to describe the apartments and rooms of strangers in minute detail, travelling, he claimed, in his mind to the addresses he was given, entering the properties and walking around the rooms. On countless occasions he was told that he was wrong, that a small brass bell was not on a certain piece of furniture, that the curtains in a drawing room were not of red velvet, but invariably he was then proved right, a maid having placed the brass bell on the piece of furniture when the owner was out, a wife changing the curtains as a surprise for her husband.

Like many other clairvoyants Didier claimed that his powers would be immediately diminished if a hardened sceptic was present. Sceptics, he believed, desensitised his powers by their determined negative thoughts.

Performing clairvoyants are always somehow suspect, for obvious reasons; even Didier's claim that sceptics could upset him might be interpreted as an advance defence in case of failure, so when a highly respectable member of society claims to be clairvoyant and proves it, weight is added to the many arguments against determined non believers.

Johann Heinrich Daniel Zcshokke (1771–1848) was such a

man, a German, born at Magdeburg; he was a playwright, a lecturer, and finally opened a boarding school at Richenau. In 1799 he settled in Aarau where he became a member of the Great Council. His books include histories of Bavaria and Switzerland and he edited a Sunday periodical expounding rationalism with eloquence and zeal. His collected writings on various subjects fill thirty-five volumes.

In his autobiography he recounts that when in the company of strangers he would know instantly their past history, where they lived, their anxieties and, their problems. When he questioned them as to whether he was right, he found that he was indeed always correct.

Once a young man irritated him somewhat by criticising the Swiss way of life, suggesting that behind their ever honest facade lay areas of hypocritical criminality. Zcshokke raised an eyebrow and asked the man whether he was one to talk. Had he not, quite recently, opened a money box belonging to his employer which was on a table to the right of the office door, and placed his hand therein to take something out? The young man was astounded, for he had been guilty of this petty thieving.

Often clairvoyant awareness can be triggered off by the sight, sound or feel of something tangible, as in psychometry, the difference being that it is not only the object in hand that helps the clairvoyant but his own ability to travel directly to the place that matters.

In 1960, a Mr Kordon-Veri in Czechoslovakia, was given the photograph of someone totally unknown to him. He was able to depict immediately the region where the photo had been taken, indicated that the person in the photo was ill and was in that particular region because of illness. The words *Velebit* and *Rabe* came to mind and he declared that the person was dying, dying at that very moment, and pronounced that in fact she had died while he was talking. This proved to be true.

The photograph was of a person staying in the Velebit Hotel on the Island of Rab on the Adriatic.

CLAIRVOYANCE IN CZECHOSLOVAKIA

Czechoslovaks, for some reason, are more advanced than others in the field of clairvoyance, possibly because there is a psychic phenomenon which is generally accepted as part of normal human development and not a lunatic idea.

In 1919, the Czechoslovak army used clairvoyants for military intelligence.

'We used clairvoyancy to great advantage in the campaign against the Hungarians,' a Czech army officer stated in a report published in a Psychic magazine. 'We'd put soldiers wth psychic ability into a trance and they'd tell us exactly the position of the Hungarian army, help us locate soldiers we'd lost, and so on. I'll never forget one occasion when a psychic said, 'I see Hungarians right now! About three hundred of them bathing in the river and poorly guarded.' He gave us the location and we set out and captured the whole unit of nude Hungarians.'

One of the pioneers of Czech paranormal research was the famous sculptor Bretislav Kafka. Wealthy because of his work, he invested much time and money in his hobby, developing psychically sensitive people into super minds.

In 1925 he picked a number of his top psychics to monitor Roald Amundsen's North Pole expedition using clairvoyant techniques. They watched with their 'second sight' the explorer's progress as though on a television screen, reporting on how bad things were going because of the fearful weather – a fact that no one else in the South could possibly know about. As Amundsen abandoned his goal because of blizzards and snow storms, Kafka's psychics reported it to the world – which, of course, took little notice.

In the Second World War, Kafka's clairvoyant team were used to find out the movements of German troops and, more importantly, to get news of relatives who had been interned by the Nazis in distant concentration camps. The Germans, hearing of this, immediately put a stop to all parapsychological research, but under Communism today it is more than ever active. Every branch of psychical research is now openly studied in Czechoslovakia, including even alchemy, reincarnation, studies with mediums, spiritualism, poltergeists and hauntings, no stone in the supernatural being left unturned.

Two women parapsychology researchers, have made important inroads into the development of this scene behind the curtain. Sheila Ostrander, a graduate of the University of Manitoba, Canada, and Lynn Schroeder, a graduate of Skidmore College, USA, both spent eight years delving into the work going on in Soviet countries, and one of their many reports, on Dr Milan Ryzl, of Prague, pinpoints the type of progress that can be made on persons who have hardly shown signs of psychic capabilities but who are keen on their own development in this field.

Milan Ryzl, working in the Prague Extra Sensory Perception laboratory, carried out experiments with his secretary, Josefka, a girl in her twenties. Getting her to agree that, together, they would try to determine whether a prophesied event could be changed, he got her to foresee an event under hypnosis involving a close friend of hers. In a trance Josefka concentrated on her friend who lived some fifty miles away and soon she visualized a quite startling scene.

She saw her friend in a restaurant with a strange man, she then saw her leaving the restaurant and getting onto the man's motorbike.

Both drove out to the country and in a deserted lane they stopped. She saw them engaging in a quarrel which escalated to a violent scene, then to her horror she saw the man rip off the girl's dress, drag her to a field and rape her.

Unable to help, in her hypnotic vision, she witnessed the fearfulness of her friend's experience.

On coming out of the trance Josefka was naturally unsettled, but considered that what she had seen was only a nightmare. For twenty-four hours she did nothing, but under the insistence of Ryzl, she rang up her friend, the idea being to forewarn her of the event which Ryzl considered might be a premonition.

As she was recounting her trance-dream to her friend, Josefka was interrupted. The friend simply told her that what she was recounting had in fact happened the night before.

A quick calculation of the time revealed that Josefka, incredibly, had been witness to her friend's abduction and rape at the very time it was happening: she had clairvoyantly travelled, first finding her friend in the restaurant, then following her on the motorcycle drive, then standing by in her state of trance while her friend was being molested.

Ryzl insists that any form of psychic sense must be considered an asset. Some months after the rape nightmare and under his tuition, Josefka clairvoyantly searched for some keys she had lost. Under hypnosis again, Ryzl urged her to go back in time and re-live the moment when she might have lost her keys. Josefka saw a clear image of her grandmother taking the keys out of her purse and placing them inside a cupboard. There was no reason why she should do this except that the old woman thought they would be safer there. On awakening, Josefka went to her flat, opened the cupboard and found the keys where she had seen her grandmother put them in the vision.

On another occasion, according to Ostrander and Schroeder, Josefka was anxious to get hold of her mother. She phoned home, but there was no answer. 'Concentrate,' Ryzl commanded, 'and tell me the precise moment when you sense that your mother is going to get in.' Josefka watched clairvoyantly, saw her mother arrive home, and phoned her. 'Why hello,' her mother answered, 'I've just come through the door.'

Ryzl has a file of cases full of precisely documented Extra Sensory Perception experiments, enough to make him the best known parapsychologist behind the Iron Curtain.

One of the best examples of travelling clairvoyancy is probably Ingo Swann, a New York artist who, in 1973, was challenged to display his powers by sceptical colleagues of two physicists at Stanford Research Institute who had been impressed by Swann's paranormal capabilities. According to Brian Inglis in *The*

Paranormal, Swann, while in the Stanford Research laboratory, was asked to describe what he could 'see' at a certain place; the only information which he was given was the precise latitude and longitude; and to ensure that he had not performed the barely credible feat of knowing what maps would reveal to anybody who had taken the trouble to learn all the co-ordinates, the world over, off by heart, he was asked to give details which maps would not show, of a place 3,000 miles away. He did, at the same time drawing a rough sketch indicating where there were buildings, a road, a fence and trees. 'Not only was Swann's description correct in every detail,' the challengers had to concede, 'but even the relative distances on his map were to scale.' To perform such a feat once would alone have strained the 'coincidence' explanation beyond credibility; but Swann was able to pass such tests time and again.

In his autobiography *Powers That Be*, the writer Beverley Nichols recalls an example of unexpected clairvoyance.

Requested by the Canadian Broadcasting Company to talk on British royalty from London, Nichols decided he would end his word picture of the Queen with a description of her driving down the Mall outside Buckingham Palace in her golden coach, flanked by her Horse Guards.

He was confidently into this fictitious description when ' . . . without any warning, I had a sharp feeling of discomfort, almost of nausea, accompanied by an acute headache. The picture of the Queen and her cavalcade vanished as swiftly as if it had been blacked out in a theatrical performance, to be replaced by an equally vivid picture of President Kennedy driving in an open car, flanked by his escort of motor bicyclists with their snarling exhausts. And, as though it were being dictated to me, I began to describe the scene . . . '

The Kennedy scene happened to fit the producer's theme, as Nichols could contrast the elaborate security precautions surrounding the President with the relatively insignificant ones then thought necessary for the Queen. The broadcast over, producer and Nichols left happily for a drink when ' . . . a little man with a white face turned the corner. He came to a halt in front of us. He stared at us, not quite seeing us. "President Kennedy," he blurted out, "has been assassinated six minutes ago." '

In this clairvoyant vision Nichols had seen President Kennedy in New York, not in Dallas, as though from a window high up in an apartment block. He recalled having seen such a cavalcade in New York a while before, agreed that while thinking of the Queen's procession it was natural that the American one should come to mind, but he couldn't explain his terrible feeling of anxiety which was *clearly recorded in his voice on the tape*.

There have been countless stories of precognition and clairvoyance surrounding the Kennedy assassination, and this is just one of them. Most are written off as coincidence, like a friend of mine recently said, rather too casually, that she had foreseen the Mexico City earthquake, but then probably often 'thought' about earthquakes and situated them in her mind in Latin American countries because that is where they are most likely to happen.

Clairvoyance always relates like coincidence, and it must be born in mind that perhaps coincidence is the enemy of paranormal reporting.

Clairvoyance is the psychic sensing of events and objects rather than thoughts. In the majority of books on the subject, sightings are often termed 'hallucinations' which suggests that the writers, though wanting to believe in the human capability of clairvoyancy, cannot accept it without a signed statement from whatever scientific body they might respect, and side step the issue. I believe that clairvoyants see what others cannot see and that it really does not matter if there is a scientific explanation or not. The clairvoyant's report must be judged on circumstances and integrity – scientific explanations and theories should come later.

It also seems to me that unless a large number of people are prepared to ignore the sceptics and just get on with experimenting, trying, probing, paranormal activities will never get off the ground.

Having said which I now suggest you try and test your own clairvoyant powers.

CLAIRVOYANT SIGHTINGS

There are three categories of clairvoyant sightings:

1 Those which are connected with the dying.
2 Those which are seen at the same time, but independently, by a number of people.
3 Those which are seen by different people but always in the same place.

The most common of these is the first, of which there are hundreds of examples. Such an experience is probably the first sign anyone may get that they are clairvoyant.

Sightings connected with the dying

1a   A young man standing in a post office queue to send a parcel greeted an elderly lady whom he knew reasonably well standing in another queue. He was surprised to see how unwell she looked and certainly older than when he had last seen her, but thought little about it. Having dealt with his parcel he moved towards the old lady to speak to her, but she turned and went out of the post office without noticing him. He mentioned the failed encounter later to a friend only to learn that the woman had actually died several days earlier.

1b   Brought up in Boston from the age of two by parents who had left England for America when they were young, a seventeen-year-old girl looked up from her book one night while reading in bed to see an old man standing by the door. From photographs she immediately recognized her grandfather whom she had never met. The vision disappeared and, a few days later, the girl learned that her grandfather had died, but just before doing so had spent his last harrowing days bemoaning the fact that he would never see his only grandchild – herself.

These two examples are known as spontaneous clairvoyancy –
sightings out of the control of the clairvoyant. Those that follow
are similar, but triggered off by a telepathy that affects a group of
people independently.

Independent sightings

2a   A nervously disposed middle aged housewife decided to visit
her son one afternoon without telling him, following a telephone
call from him informing her that he intended to leave his wife and
get a divorce. So upset was she by this unexpected domestic
development that she missed her train and abandoned her visit for
that day. Her son and his new girl friend, however, both saw her
crossing the road and coming towards their block of flats,
recognizing her by the dark green corduroy slacks she always
wore with a matching kerchief. She never got to the flat, of
course, because she was not in the vicinity that afternoon, but the
son and his girl friend saw her as a vision created by her intention
to see them.

2b   At nine o'clock one morning in a busy city office three
secretaries independently saw their boss arrive, hang his coat and
hat on his office peg and sit down at his desk. They saw him
through the partition window, each sitting at their own work in
the typist pool. A few seconds later a director of the company
came in to inform them that the man in question had suffered a
near fatal accident and was in hospital. All three reacted in the
same way, claiming they had just seen him come in, but on
checking realized that his coat and his hat were not where they
thought they had seen him hang them.

Later, the boss confirmed that on being knocked down and
travelling to the hospital in the ambulance he had had only one
thing on his mind – getting to the office on time to be a good
example to his staff.

Sightings in the same place

Category 3 concerns sightings by different clairvoyants but which are always in the same place, lending weight to stories that a site is haunted. The following, from Eysenck and Sargent's *Explaining the Unexplained* is in fact quoted as a typical 'haunting'.

> I had lived in Trondheim, Norway, for four years and left the city in 1938, but have often visited the city since that time. I was much interested in the construction work done at the cathedral. One sunny morning I went into the cathedral. I walked along the north passage. Looking across towards the south hall, I noticed a nun sitting quietly in one of the many niches along the wall. I wondered what she was doing here at this time of day. I thought I would talk to her as I came closer, but when I was just six or seven feet away from her, she faded away and I saw her no more! I must say I was puzzled, but walking into the west end of the cathedral I stopped and talked to one of the women cleaning the church and said to her, 'I thought I saw a Catholic nun over in the west end, sitting in a niche, but when I came near she disappeared. How could that be?' 'Oh,' answered the woman, 'We often see her.' And this I had verified by others.

An anxiety trace?

Why do they always have to be cathedrals or old rectories and nuns or priests or monks? I would suggest that hauntings, that is to say clairvoyant sightings, occur everywhere at anytime, but only those who live in cloistered surroundings, who have *time* to think about the details of their daily lives, are the ones who *record* such occurrences. If you live in a busy city, would you *know* a ghost if you saw one? How many are there walking our streets, crossing on zebra crossings in a hurry to catch that bus that they may have missed? How many times in a week do we in fact have a 'strange' experience and shrug it off because there is no *time* to think about it, and then it is forgotten.

Ghost stories belong to the past because clairvoyants had time to see apparitions, had time to reflect on the odd occurrence in their life, there wasn't much else going on. But now? If you saw a friend waving at you from a passing vehicle and later learned that he had died that morning, would you remember the precise time when you saw him? 'That's a bit odd,' you might comment, 'I only saw him the other day waving from a car . . . can't remember exactly when it was . . . I was rushing home to catch "Dallas" . . . was it Thursday? Tuesday? The day of the World Cup, the day one of the Apollo's misfired again . . . ' Who knows? Who *cares*? And so an opportunity of discovering a paranormal faculty is missed.

DEVELOPING CLAIRVOYANT POWERS

So, can clairvoyancy be developed?

If you believe Milan Ryzl, it can be.

How?

Whether learning a new language, a new craft, or training yourself to do something you have never done before, it is all a question of technique, patience and effort. Unlike learning how to ride a bicycle, drive a car or use a computer, however, clairvoyancy is a natural faculty within you which has to be brought out, *then* worked on.

To begin with, therefore, you must teach yourself to get a clear vision of the normal (as opposed to paranormal) things going on around you, you must train yourself to become observant, and practise conscious visualization.

To test your observational powers, kick off by looking for five minutes or so at a painting or a photograph, put it away, then try to reproduce it in your mind. Afterwards, check to see what you remembered, or rather what you have forgotten.

If you repeat this test often with different paintings you will automatically find the way that suits you best to remember everything. It may be that you pan the picture from left to right with a mental commentary of what you are seeing: window, curtains, table under window, carpet under table, waste paper basket near table leg, etc. Or you may find it easier to pull back from the picture like a film camera staring at the centre and filling the surroundings clockwise: oak tree centre, clouds at one, hills at two, cottage on hill at three, cows in front of cottage at four, stream at five and so on . . .

Or you might prefer to study the scene from afar and zoom in onto details, or simply stare and stare at it for a long time and later discover that a subconscious eye is taking it all in and that the mind has recorded it for you without you being aware of making any effort.

If this is the case, you are fortunately a natural visualizer – of which there are many – and may not need too much preparative work.

Once you are satisfied that you 'know' how to observe, the very best pre training for travelling clairvoyance is to travel and take in your surroundings again.

All of us travel daily, some great distances by train or bus or car, others very short distances from bedroom to bathroom to kitchen sink, but we are moving and we are passing all sorts of objects on the way.

Before going to sleep, or before fully waking up, make that familiar journey again and again in your mind. Travel from A to B and back again and, like you did with the painting, go over the same ground in reality and check what you missed out. After a while you will see that you automatically take in everything, that you are a natural visualizer.

Now what you are going to aim at in travelling clairvoyance is a very similar journey to the one you make lying in your bed re-visualizing the daily journey you make – only it will be to somewhere you have never been to before.

Choose a place you know about but have never been to, a friend's house which you have never visited, the high street of a neighbouring village you have not in fact been to, then, using one of the psychic screens suggested below, *travel* to that house, down that high street, and later go there in reality.

Bear in mind, however, that you will not achieve this transportation of the mind in one day, nor indeed in one month. It will take you a very long time to achieve that sort of 'on command' clairvoyance – but achieve it you can.

However ridiculous the following may sound, please bear with these suggestions for they do help. Let people laugh if they find out what you are up to, or preferably do all this in secret, but do not write off the rituals proposed as silly, for *ritual* – which all of us practise every day in one form or another – is the key to concentration, and concentration with any form of psychic experiment is essential.

From the moment we get up in the morning till we go to bed at night we follow certain rituals, though we may not realize it. There is the breakfast ritual, the saying goodbye 'I'm off to the office now' ritual, the arrival at work ritual, and the settling down to work ritual.

Observe people in restaurants, sitting at the ready laid table. They will move a glass, a fork, adjust the plates, move their spectacles up their nose or down their nose to study the menu with a cough, all of which is unnecessary, except that it is a form of preparation for an important act to come. It is ritual. Smokers have a ritual, the whole business of extricating the cigarette from the pack, finding the lighter, placing the cigarette in the mouth, lighting it. Drinkers have drinking rituals, sex maniacs no doubt have their rituals, and certainly all churches and religious services depend on ritual to get the congregation's attention – the rosary just to mention one example.

What makes the following ritual sound banal is that the objects mentioned in connection with a clairvoyant sitting have been laughed at in comic books and movies for years because they belong to the bell, book and candle brigade – to witches, wizards, sorcerers, mediums and spiritualists.

I am talking about their accoutrements – the crystal ball, the ink pool, the black mirror and the sand circle.

All of which will help you visualize where your travelling clairvoyancy is taking you by concentrating the images and helping you to interpret them as reality.

These objects, it must be stressed, have absolutely no powers in themselves, but are psychic screens into which your supernatural perceptions can be focussed from the subconscious levels of your mind.

Crystal balls can be purchased in toy shops and joke shops. These are usually made of acrylic plastic and will scratch easily, but they are better than nothing. The ideal is to buy a real crystal, from psychic orientated shops (usually selling books on the supernatural) or better still finding an old crystal ball in an antique or junk shop.

Crystal balls should be wrapped in silk, kept away from strong light and set down in ebony. I doubt if any of this really matters unless it is part of your own personal ritual. I own a crystal ball (actually given me by a dying Godmother who was a failed medium but a successful faith healer) and this, I keep wrapped in blue velvet and house in a pine box. Opening the lid and lifting it out with care and setting it down on its carved ivory base gives me a feeling of great pleasure, and certainly the sensation that I am handling something of very great value which may hold the key to all sorts of perceptions – which is what ritual should trigger off. When holding this ball I become a wizard with psychic powers and I may just as well be holding the Royal Orb.

The ink pool is my own favourite; it is a method of clairvoyant visualization favoured in the Middle East. You gaze down into this bowl of dark liquid and, providing there are no distracting reflections, you can lose yourself in the depths of this bottomless magic well for hours.

Black mirrors have to be made, and they are virtually just one facet of the crystal ball. First, find an old clock with a circular face protected by a circular convex glass (junk shops are full of them), open the convex window, paint the inside with black enamel paint, close the new black window and you have a black mirror.

The sand circle is simplest. Purchase a sheet of sand-paper, cut it in the form of a circle, about six inches in diameter, paint it dark blue or black, preferably with ink or water colour paints (gloss or matt paints tend to obliterate the sparkle of the sand grains which lend that quality of depth necessary for concentration,) and stick it down on a piece of wood to keep its surface evenly flat.

If you prepare these objects with care and respect, and are clever enough with your hands to decorate them in order to give them the semblance of value, it all helps. You must accept that to others such ritual will be like hocus-pocus, and so it probably is, but whereas the hocus-pocus of the magician is designed to make you concentrate away from the sleight of hand, the hocus-pocus suggested here is to draw your subconscious visualization from your mind into the reflecting receptacle.

As with any other form of psychic session, you must have comfortable, loose clothing, a sitting angle that suits you, a pleasant room temperature, everything you need in its place.

You should have a tape machine or writing materials to make notes about the session close by. Recording what happened is important to find out what conditions and in which state of health you are when best results are achieved.

A chart prepared with the following headings: DATE, TIME, TEMPERATURE, WEATHER, MOON PHASE, HEALTH, REMARKS saves time and makes for clearer checking of your reports.

Obviously if you can set aside a special room or laboratory for your psychic experiments all the better, but this is not essential. Some clairvoyants go to elaborate lengths to prepare what might be called a 'temple' or 'sacred precinct', possibly furbished with meaningful pictures (zodiac signs and the like) special lighting and even joss sticks burning. The ritual of getting all this together helps of course, but if you become too dependent on such theatre you may not be able to function clairvoyantly without all such accessories. The joy of psychic power is to have total control over that power and it will slow you down if you have to rely on too many symbolic objects and atmospheres to activate yourself.

Let us now go through the first steps of a clairvoyant experiment using the ink pool.

The pool should be a bowl not less than five inches in diameter, and shallow, not more than half-an-inch deep. The shallow bowl (a soup plate, for example) should be placed exactly like a soup plate before you at a table, but you should be seated so that you can look straight down into it, comfortably.

Make sure that any lights are not reflected in the pool, blue shaded lights are best, or green, *not* red which tends to negate the darkness and depth of the pool.

Stare down into the liquid.

The pool, after a short while will seem to go out of focus and you will start sensing pins and needles down the length of your nose, between the eyes and perhaps feel a tightness around your head. These are normal physical sensations which you would feel if, say, you were sewing or painting a miniature or making a model which needs little movement. Nothing supernatural has yet occurred, only your physical body is getting accustomed to this new stance.

The first sign of paranormal activity is a dimness on the surface of the ink pool, then a clouding over of the black depth to which you should now have become accustomed.

Crystal gazers in fantasy stories invariably see their glass spheres clouding over. Films show Madame Arkatis staring wide eyed as magical clouds mist up their vision. This actually is not the invention of bright scriptwriters, it is taken from fact. Crystal balls at this stage do seem to cloud over, black mirrors mist up, ink pools go grey and sand circles tend to sparkle – a much more dramatic and rewarding effect.

You may at this point start seeing flashes of light in your psychic screen. It is vital that you should not allow yourself to cry victory and become excited. It *is* the first sign of a clairvoyancy breakthrough, but any wild nervous reaction on your part will virtually destroy what you have achieved so far. Remain calm, passive, and go on staring into the pool as though such an occurrence was perfectly normal.

During the next stage you really must try to disassociate your everyday self from what you are experiencing because it is extremely exciting and magical, far more than when you first saw a picture on a new television screen or a polaroid photograph coming out before your very eyes for the first time.

Within the confines of the ink pool you will start seeing faces, images, landscapes and bright colours. They will appear and disappear meaninglessly, but they will be there, as they so often are in your mind but concentrated now within the framework of your psychic screen.

These pictures cannot be seen by anyone else but you, they are projected images from your subconscious and are only different from those you see daily in half sleep because you have channelled them into the receptacle.

Now when you have mastered the difficult art of holding onto just one of these images long enough to study it – and this I must emphasize may take *months* rather than days – you must then learn to interpret the images as you interpret your dreams.

INTERPRETING THE IMAGES

There are two types of image reflected in the psychic screen by your subconscious.

1   Images which are in no way connected with you.
2   Images which are directly connected with you.

Checking emotional reactions when discovering which is which is a step you have to take great pains to master.

It is like standing behind your own front door waiting for the postman to deliver a much desired letter.

You stare at the blank door for a long time waiting patiently for the letter to pop through the letter box, then, unexpectedly, the door opens. In the street before you people are passing by – they have nothing to do with you – you know that instinctively, but then you see a postman and you get excited. He must be coming towards you, to your house, with your letter. But he does not. He passes by on the other side and the disappointment can be so shattering that you automatically close the door. But what if you are closing the door in another postman's face? He may be so vexed that he never bothers to deliver the letter he has for you. The first postman may not be your postman. The first images may not be your images. So be patient, wait, reflect, until one image is suddenly and quite clearly meaningful to you.

Never allow yourself to be disappointed when pictures which appear have no direct connection. Eventually they will, and only if you *record precisely* what you have seen during your sessions will certain images become meaningful because you will realize that you have manufactured your own symbols – not symbols for anyone else, but symbols for yourself.

For example: a spider seen in the morning is a symbol of bad luck, in the evening good luck – to some people anyway. Comets are omens of misfortune, the new moon a sign of good fortune. These are superstitions.

But you must not be sidetracked by believing that if you see a spider, a comet or a new moon in your psychic screen they have any connection with those superstitions. What is important is for you to feel that a certain image means something to you. Note it down, and if it is repeated again and again and you have filled out your report sheet dutifully, you will see a pattern emerge and symbols from your very own subconscious will tell you something, convey a message.

One clairvoyant early on got the very clear image of a white horse galloping down a deserted air strip. By making notes and recording everything that happened around the time he saw this recurring vision, he soon realized that the galloping white horse meant that his daughter was on her way to visit him, or was about to ring, or was writing him a letter. When, one day, he saw the vision of the deserted air strip without the horse he felt understandably anxious. He acted on his anxiety, rang her up and learned that she had had an accident, was in hospital and urgently wanted to see him.

113

WORKING WITHOUT THE SCREEN

Once you have mastered the art of clairvoyancy by using your psychic screen, you must then learn to do without it, which is fairly simple.

Sitting in exactly the same room in the same position with the same light intensity and temperature, open up your clairvoyant session with whatever ritual works best for you, but all *without* the ink pool, sand circle, crystal ball or black mirror.

The images, you will find, project themselves where the 'screen' used to be, and you will then realize that your visions were never in fact in the ink pool, but in your mind.

Having practised long enough getting these visions in your mind, you may then enter the dangerous phase of clairvoyancy, unless you learn to *switch off*.

If this proves difficult it is because you are enjoying yourself too much and are over indulging in your new power, but if you fail to switch off, by simply looking away, moving away, switching on brighter lights and immediately doing something physical, you may find that you have no control over your clairvoyancy and that it will flare up with an unexpected vision when you least need it – for instance when you are driving a car at speed, using a sharp knife, or walking an innocent child across a dangerous street.

You have now become a more responsible person with the extra power of an added faculty, and this must be respected and not abused.

The best way to switch off when you wish is to have something practical to do after your session, and one of the best things that can occupy your mind is to write up your notes, or record them on tape.

Do not take the dog out for a walk, or think that by going shopping for the week's provisions you will switch off. The clairvoyant mind hangs onto its images for a long time: walking does not help switch off, it encourages day dreaming – so do something diverting.

114

USING CLAIRVOYANT POWERS

What, you may now ask, can you do with your new clairvoyant powers? To what good purpose can you put them? If you have not already worked this out for yourself, I will suggest a few.

You can watch over those for whom you care.

You can become the best security guard in the business.

You can seek and search for missing persons.

You can seek and search for valuables mislaid.

You can travel ahead of a proposed journey to check that all is well where you intend going. (Is your holiday hotel as ideal as described in the brochure?)

You can become evil and plan bank raids, terrorist raids, assassinations and vile crimes.

You can spy, politically, industrially, militarily.

You can become a peeping Tom.

What you will not be able to do is see into the future because though you have learned to project your mind's eye into other areas of reality, you cannot project it forward through time.

That category of clairvoyancy is reserved for the *precognitive* clairvoyants whom I find as fascinating as I believe improbable, but to whom I will all the same devote the next section because, though no proof has come my way that what they foresee is in fact foreseeable, it very well may be. Soon.

MEDIUMS AND SPIRITUALISTS

Mediums and spiritualists have to be classified as clairvoyant, though I personally have certain doubts as to the credibility of this particular psychic power and cannot offer suggestions as to how to contact the life hereafter. But because I have doubts, it certainly does not mean that I should not examine the claims made by the large number of people who daily make contact with the dead. Over and above everything I believe in leaving all doors wide open until they are slammed rudely in one's face by undeniable negative evidence.

There are two categories of medium, 'physical mediums' and 'intellectual mediums', both of whom claim to possess the type of psychic power which enables them to communicate with those who have 'passed over'.

The physical medium does this by getting the dead to make contact by physical means, that is by moving tables, objects, rattling cutlery, banging doors or, most frightening of all, manifesting themselves in the form of ectoplasm – 'Something moulded or formed' according to the Oxford English Dictionary. The *Encyclopedia of the Unexplained* dwells on it at greater length, however:

> . . . in Spiritualist belief, the substance from which spirits make themselves visible forms. It is said to be extruded from some Mediums, and is described as alive, sensitive to touch and light – if it is unexpectedly touched or a light is suddenly shone on it, it flies back into the Medium's body, sometimes causing injury – cold to the touch, slightly luminous and having a characteristic smell. Whether such a substance exists and (if it does) what it is made of, has never been satisfactorily determined.

The intellectual medium hears the voices of the dead, can sometimes project the voice through his or her own, and certainly holds conversations with the deceased which is much like listening to a person talking on the telephone – you can only guess at what is being said the other end.

Mediums very often use guides to help them contact the other world and, like crystal balls and tea leaves, they tend to have become comical due mainly to the strange names given them by the mediums and their apparent provence. Red Indians abound, as well as Chinese, Aztecs, and Mexicans, with such names as Little White Hawk, Lee Ping, Atahuelpito, Juanito or, sometimes, a more acceptable and plain Mary-Jane.

The most famous mediums in history were the Fox sisters who, in 1848, opened up the flood gates of psychic interest in America.

The daughters of a Methodist farmer, they lived in the small town of Arcadia, Wayne County, NY, in a wooden house, and on the night of March 31 of that year Margarette, 14, and Catherine, 12, gained control over a series of mysterious knockings that had been disturbing the household for months.

The noises were eventually diagnosed as rapped messages from the dead which, translated in our terms, told the girls that a man had been murdered in the house and had been buried in the cellar.

When neighbours dug up the cellar floor, human remains were found and from then on the Fox sisters and their mother could go nowhere without spirits catching up with them, giving them messages and making them news headlines across the country.

To support the claims of mediums, I list the more famous ones which are mentioned in most books on the subject:

Winifred Coombe-Tennant (1874–1956)
Alice Fleming (Mrs Holland) (1868–1948) Rudyard Kipling's sister.
Eileen Garrett (1893–1970)
D.D. Howe (1833–1866)
Gladys Leonard (1882–1968)
Leonora Piper (1857–1968)
Eusepio Palladino (1854–1918)
Ann Verrall (1858–1916)
Helen Verrall (1883–1959) her daughter.
Last but by no means least, because she is the most famous of all mediums and influenced a great many people to study the art of spiritualism – Helena Petrova Blavatsky (1831–1891).

I would point out a strange but obvious fact – out of the twelve mediums mentioned above, eleven are women.

Gladys Leonard

This medium spent a childhood of visions. She never mentioned them to her parents, lived with her sightings under control till she was in her twenties and only then discovered that she was psychic.

Studying the subject she developed into a controlled medium and made contact with a guide whom she called 'Feda' (an Indian girl!). This child from the world beyond relayed messages to

117

friends and relatives of deceased persons to Gladys Leonard, who relayed them to the families concerned during spiritualistic seances.   In A.T. Baird's *One Hundred Cases for Survival After Death*, is a recorded typescript of a sitting with Gladys Leonard, held on behalf of a Mr Blair, during which Feda contacted the recently deceased Mrs Blair. (Mr Blair's comments added later are in brackets.)

This lady (Mrs Blair?) died in the prime of life.
(She was 37 years of age.)
She was not fussy or shouted much.
(She was a woman of strong but restrained character.)
She had an exhausted feeling of death. It happened within five days.
(Correct as stated.)
Until the illness came she had a strong constitution.
(She had been well for the greater part of her life.)
Before she died he (Mr Blair?) tried to do something on a Monday. He did not succeed. He tried to see important people but failed. H and M are the letters connected with them.
(I returned home on the Monday before Mrs Blair died. I found her seriously ill. We went to a specialist that day and a minor operation was performed without beneficial results. Later I called in Dr M. and wanted to get a Dr H., but didn't.
Her thoughts go to a man and her daughter.
(We have three daughters.)
She is anxious to get in touch with F.B.
(My initials.)
The man (F.B.) has something to do with an office.
(I am a lawyer and of course have an office.)
This lady's ancestors were not ordinary people.
(The Lorens – my wife's folks – were definitely not ordinary people. She had some outstanding ancestors.)
She speaks of a Charlie.
(Her brother.)
He (F.B.) is closely linked with a big institution.
(I am Director of Works in my State.)
He's been doing something special lately, signing his name, something big.
(The oath of office of Director of Public Works is signed in a large book in the Comptroller's office.)
He is at the top of this institute, a leader.
(See previous remarks)

He was photographed much and didn't like it.

(The press took pictures of my being sworn in by the new Comptroller and I didn't like it.)

He's had special, unusual clothes, lately.

(I think this refers to my honorary degree. I dressed up in an academic cap and gown.)

He has lots of people before him. They listen to him like the Day of Judgement. They want his opinion.

(See previous remarks)

He has something to seal.

(Seals are relevant to a lawyer's business.)

Is he fond of music?

(Doubtful)

He has at last realized what we both talked over so often.

(Correct)

He has got more money lately but is careless about it.

(There has been a more or less favourable turn in my investments. I do not think about money – probably not as much as I should.)

He was doing something big connected with a platform.

(The honorary degree was conferred on a platform)

Was he connected with invalids or cripples in some big way?

(I am Trustee for a hospital for crippled children.)

Eusepio Palladino

Born in Naples and orphaned early on, Eusepio Palladino was adopted by a family who were fond of dabbling with the occult and held seances often. During these sittings she revealed that she has psychic capabilities. When she attended them the family realized that lights flashed in the room, a guitar twanged and the table moved of its own accord.

Her powers became known to Charles Richet, the French physiologist and Nobel Prize winner, and he carried out a number of tests on her, which proved satisfactory. She was then tested again by three sceptical investigators working in the parapsychological field – Everard Fielding, Hereward Carrington and W.W. Baggally. Carrington, an amateur magician, was hell bent on finding out how Palladino did her tricks, and below follows the report of their tests from Everard Fielding's book, *Sitting with Eusepio Palladino and Other Studies*:

The experimental room was part of the living quarters of the investigators in Naples. It had a rectangular table set close to one of the corners of the room. This corner was partitioned off by a curtain to form a small cabinet. The medium sat at one end of the table with her back to the cabinet. Usually two of the investigators would sit on either side of her, the third often facing her from the other side of the table. Inside the cabinet usually, was a small table with several objects on it. The floor of the cabinet was made of tiles closely cemented together. One of the walls was of thick masonry and faced the street, the other was the wall to Baggally's bedroom. There were no doors or opening to the cabinet other than through the curtain. Occasionally, others took part in the tests, usually Italian investigators. The lights were dimmed but there was enough illumination to see the medium during the major occurrences.

During the eleven sessions, a total of 470 ostensibly paranormal phenomena were recorded, 305 of these when the arms and legs of the medium were observed or held by two of the members of the committee of the Society for Psychical Research and 144 when she was controlled in this way by an SPR member and another investigator. Among the incidents in the former group, on thirty-four occasions the table round which the investigators and the medium were sitting, levitated completely from the floor. For instance, on one occasion, the table lifted off the ground, with all four legs off in full light, while Baggally and Carrington were watching the hands and legs (or rather long dress) of the medium and while Baggally had his right hand across her two knees. Fifty nine times there were bulgings and movements of the curtains behind the medium, twenty-eight times there were movements of objects – other than the table – outside the cabinet. Forty two times the SPR investigators were grasped or touched by a hand or some other tangible object either through the curtain or outside the curtain. Thus when Baggally was watching the medium's hands and was holding them separately in his hands, another hand , apparently a materialized one, grasped his arm and touched him in other places. Baggally ruled out the possibility that it might be the medium's foot that had grasped him in this way or that anyone else in the seance room had done it. He was 'driven to the conclusion' (preposterous though it appears to me) that the supernormal force, which had given me conclusive evidence of its existence through the phenomena previously described, was able to produce the effects of tangible matter and assume the form of a hand.

Fielding, Carrington and Baggally finally formed the opinion after all their tests were carried out that, 'A large proportion of the manifestations of which we were witness in Naples were clearly beyond the possibilities of any conceivable form of conjuring.'

I have reproduced the above two reports simply to give you an idea of what mediums are reputed to have achieved.

There are many such reports in books and documents on the subject. I personally believe that phenomena appearing at seances are real, that mediums are capable of moving mountains, of telling you what dead relatives are saying but that, like the ouija and like the Tarots and like any other form of determined contact with another form of life, all the answers come from within us, through telepathy from our own subconscious through to the subconsciousness of the medium who is able to transform the information into very dramatic representations, and our minds are so extraordinary that they are even capable of making us believe that we can see into the future.

8
PRECOGNITION

Certain knowledge of a future event seems to me impossible. All other forms of the paranormal mentioned in this book are based on what our subconscious state can imbibe and put to further use, but nothing our conscious or subconscious states can take in can belong to what is not already in existence.

Precognition, premonitions, divination, fortune telling and astrology all tend to be put in the same bag – that of an ability to foretell the future.

We all want to do this so much, or want others to do it for us, that we are ready on too many occasions, to believe that psychics have this power.

They do not.

They cannot.

What they do have is perhaps a very deep understanding of how to manipulate their own, and other people's, minds and interpret the questions asked to their satisfaction.

ASTROLOGY, misinterpreted daily in the press under Zodiac signs and telling millions of people born on a certain date that they are all going to experience the same good fortune or the same fearful disaster, is in fact a science devoted to discovering the hidden laws which govern the universe.

DIVINATION is a guessing game, nothing more: whether using cards, tea leaves, bumps on the head, palmistry or our old friend the crystal ball, divination relies on people's credulity and gullibility. There is no basis for it. How can one possibly know for certain what is going to happen tomorrow? All of us can guess, very often correctly, but surely we cannot *know* for sure.

PREMONITIONS are hunches or intuitive guesses as to what may be about to happen, usually based on unsettling feelings. It is rare that one hears of a pleasant premonition, indeed it is rare to hear of any valid premonition at all.

Nostradamus (1503-1568) can claim to be the most famous of all prophets, but only due to his *Almanac and Prognostications*, published annually when he was alive. His *'Centaines'*, a book of prophecies divided into ten sections of ten quatrains, in old French, are rhyming views of the future, the majority of which are obscure enough to be misinterpreted any way you wish. The end of the world appears a number of times, depending on what date you can set various symbolic pointers. A masterly piece of work guaranteed to give you as many alternatives as you want to predict, whatever doom you wish upon the world or yourself.

At the risk of being accused of plugging my own books, I will mention here that the first psychic thriller I wrote was inspired by Nostradamus's quatrains and was entitled *Premonitions of an Inherited Mind*. In it a perfectly normal and well balanced business executive discovers at the very start of the story that he is clairvoyant – then when he later meets a seasoned psychic, he learns that he is a direct descendant of Nostradamus and has to bear the awful consequences.

The opening page, though fictitious, is an example of how precognition works and was based on a powerful dream I had which I thought perhaps was a premonition.

Central Park, New York.

11.30 on the morning of March 3rd, Michael Dartson was taking a last walk before returning to his apartment on East 76th Street to collect his hand luggage and go to the airport.

He stopped, closed his eyes and, for a moment, turned his face to the sun, then he heard a woman's voice quite distinctly.

'Don't touch that package, for God's sake don't touch it!'

He felt an area of the ground around him shudder, then fearful screams of panic enveloped him.

Ten days later it happened.'

That was my dream.

At 5.45 on Monday 13th March, Norma Dartson, unable to get a taxi in Regent Street after a tiring afternoon's shopping, joined the rush hour commuters going down the Piccadilly tube.

Holding tightly onto her handbag and gripping the top of her mink coat, she battled to get a ticket and, once through the automatic barrier machines, relaxed a little on the steps of the descending escalator, calculating that within twenty minutes or so she would be back above ground in the fresher Knightsbridge air, and soon sitting down for a hotel tea with her daughter Sarah.

As the escalator reached the bottom hallway and she was checking the indications to the various destinations, she became aware of a confusion to her right. Amid the mass of people hurrying in various directions, a group were trying to avoid something on the floor.

It was a package, neatly wrapped in brown paper, and tied with white string.

Then she saw a woman stoop to pick it up.

There was a blinding flash of blue and white light, followed by a thunderous blast.

Norma felt herself showered with icy water which then gave off unbearable heat. Putting her hand up to her face to protect it, she felt it to be sticky and she tasted. . .blood.

That was fiction, for the dream never came true, unless one wants to twist and turn in desperation to prove that it was a premonition and claim that one of the many IRA bombings that occurred in London seven weeks after I wrote it was the one I dreamt about as an omen.

To accept precognition, one must come to terms with time as a fourth dimension, and to do this it is best to launch oneself into the reading of P.D. Ouspensky, a disciple of George Ivanovich Gurdjieff, which has immersed many a person fascinated in the occult into depths of misunderstandings about our inner lives from which they have never recovered.

Enough has been written about G.I. Gurdjieff to furbish a long shelfful of volumes: suffice it to say here, that he was an exceptional Armenian who, after a lifetime of experiences in the esoteric world of mysticism, founded a school that taught man how to develop the other you. His teachings were based on the principle that man is 'asleep' and must 'awaken', that man is a creature of habit and subject to innumerable self imposed laws which make him function. He must break some of these laws to become master of himself, and this is achieved mainly by self observation to a minute degree.

Peter Demienovitch Ouspensky, was a well established journalist and lecturer on occult subjects when he met Gurdjieff whom he found more consistent in his theories than anyone else he had interviewed up till then. Ouspensky studied with Gurdjieff and documented his teaching for the rest of his life and in one of his books – *The New Model of the Universe* – he describes his own experiment in precognitive clairvoyance which I find to be the clearest explanation of how near we can get to foreseeing the future:

> During my experiments I many times attempted to 'see', for instance, when I was myself in the house, what was happening in the street, which I could not see in the natural way, or to 'see' some man or other whom I knew well, what he was doing at that moment; or to reconstruct fully scenes from the past of which I knew only some parts.
>
> Then I sealed some old photographs from an album into envelopes of the same size, mixed them up and tried to 'see' whose portrait I held in my hand. I tried the same thing with playing cards.
>
> When I became convinced that I was not succeeding, I tried to reconstruct as a clear visual image what was undoubtedly in my memory, though in the ordinary state I could not visualise it at will. For instance I tried to 'see' the Nevsky, starting from Znamensky Square, with all the houses and shop signs in their order. But this also was never successful when done intentionally.

Unintentionally and in various circumstances I more than once saw myself walking along the Nevsky, and then I 'saw' both the houses and signs exactly as they would be in reality.

Finally I had to recognize as unsuccessful all attempts to pass to concrete facts. Either it is quite impossible, or else I attempted it in the wrong way.

But there were two cases which showed that there is a possibility of a very great strengthening of our capacities of perception in relation to the ordinary events of life.

Once I obtained not exactly clairvoyance, but undoubtedly a very great strengthening of the capacity of vision. It was in Moscow in the street, half an hour after an experiment which had seemed to me to be entirely unsuccessful. For a few seconds my vision suddenly became extraordinarily acute. I could quite clearly see faces of people at a distance at which normally one would have difficulty in distinguishing one figure from another.

Another instance occurred during the second winter of my experiments in St Petersburg. Circumstances were such that the whole of that winter I was unable to go to Moscow, although at the time I very much wanted to go there in connection with several different matters. Finally I remember that about the middle of February I definitely decided that I would go to Moscow for Easter. Soon after that I again began my experiments. Once, quite accidentally, when I was in the state in which moving signs or hieroglyphs were beginning to appear, I had a thought about Moscow, or about someone whom I had to see there at Easter. Suddenly, without warning, I received the comment that I should not go to Moscow at Easter. Why? In answer to this I saw how, starting from the day of the experiment I have described, events began to develop in a definite order and sequence. Nothing new happened, but the causes, which I could see quite well and which were all there on the day of my experiment, were evolving, and having come to the results which unavoidably followed from them, they formed just before Easter a whole series of difficulties which in the end prevented me going to Moscow. The fact in itself, as I looked at it, had a merely curious character, but the interesting side of it was that I saw what looked like a possibility of calculating the future – the whole future was contained in the present. I saw that all that had happened before Easter resulted directly from what had already existed two months earlier.

Then in my experiment I probably passed on to other thoughts, and on the following day I remembered only the bare result, that 'somebody' had told me I should not go to Moscow at Easter. This was ridiculous, because I saw nothing that could prevent it. Then I forgot

126

all about my experiment. It came to my memory again only a week before Easter, when suddenly a whole succession of small circumstances were precisely those which I had 'seen' during my experiment, and they quite definitely resulted from what had existed two months before that. Nothing new had happened.

When everything fell out exactly as I had seen, or foreseen, in that strange state, I remembered my experiment, remembered all the details, remembered that I saw and knew then what had to happen.

In this incident I undoubtedly came into contact with the possibility of a different vision in the world of things and events. But, speaking generally, all the questions which I asked myself referring to real life or to concrete knowledge led to nothing.

I think this is connected with a principle which became clear to me during my experiments.

In ordinary life we think by thesis and antithesis; always and everywhere there is 'yes' or 'no', 'no' or 'yes'. In thinking differently, in thinking in a new way, in thinking by means of signs of things, I came to understand the fundamental errors of our mental process.

In reality, everywhere and in every case there were not two but three elements. There were not only 'yes' and 'no', but 'yes', 'no' and something else besides. And it was precisely the nature of this 'third' element, inaccessible to the understanding, which made all ordinary reasonings unsuitable and demanded a change in the basic method. I saw that the solution of all the problems always came from a *third*, unknown, element, that is to say, it came from a third and unknown side, and that without this third element it was impossible to arrive at a right solution.

Further, when I asked a question I very often began to see that the question itself was wrongly put. Instead of giving an immediate answer to my question, the 'consciousness' to which I was speaking began to move my question round and turn it about, showing me that it was wrong. Gradually I began to see what was wrong. As soon as I understood clearly what was wrong in my question, *I saw the answer*. But the answer always included a third element which I could not see before, because my question was always built upon two elements only, thesis and antithesis. I formulated this for myself in the following way: that the whole difficulty lay in the putting of the question. If we could put questions rightly, we would know the answers.

A question rightly put contains the answer itself. But the answer will be quite unlike what we expect, it will always be on another plane not included in the ordinary question.

In several cases in which I attempted to think with certain ready made words or with ready made ideas I experienced a strange sensation like a physical shock. Before me complete emptiness opened out, because in the real world with which I had come into contact there was nothing corresponding to these words or ideas.

When seeking the other you, it is this very sensation which Ouspensky describes as 'a complete emptiness opening out' which will give you the key to what you are looking for.

Nothing, as he says, corresponds in our subconscious to the real world with which we are in contact.

For those, by now, determined to develop themselves psychically, I would highly recommend the following four P.D. Ouspensky books.

The Psychology of Man's Possible Evolution.
In Search of the Miraculous.
The New Model of the Universe.
The Fourth Way.

9
AURAS

Subtle emanation from anything; atmosphere diffused by or attending a person etc., especially in mystical use as a definite envelope of body or spirit.

Oxford English Dictionary.

Eileen Garret, one of the twelve mediums mentioned in a previous chapter claimed that she could see spirals of energy leaving a nearly dead body. 'I've always seen every plant, animal and person encircled by a misty surround.'

The idea of an aura, a luminosity radiating from our bodies, is as old as history itself, and that all living matter is surrounded by an energy cloud, which can be seen by sensitives as a colourful emanation following the contours of the body to a width of between one centimetre and a metre, is one of the phenomena described by psychics which is accepted by scientists as being worthy of examination.

Since time immemorial holy personages have been represented by a surrounding light, and long before the Christians circled the heads of their saints with halos, the early Egyptians, the Greeks, Romans and Indians had fringes of radiancy shining from the bodies of their deities and the aura of Buddha was believed to envelope a whole city.

Not until the middle of the nineteenth century were auras questioned by science. In the 1850s the German chemist Baron Karl von Rheichenbach (1788-1869), who discovered creosote and paraffin, became interested in the paranormal and started experimenting with various psychic friends, coming to the conclusion that people radiated a force that particularly sensitive persons could see and feel in the dark. He called this force *od*, from which came the term *odic force*, a form of body magnetism which many at the time were pleased to believe explained away the root of spiritualists' ectoplasm, their power to move furniture, speak in a multitude of voices and make a good deal of frightening noises.

Though a Yugoslav scientist, Nikola Tesla, became interested in the subject some thirty years later and invented a wire coil device that caused the body to spark, it was not till 1911 that someone decided to research the possibility that this divine mythical light could in fact be explained as an electric current produced by the human body.

A British doctor, Walter Kilner (1847-1920), in charge of the electro-therapy department of St Thomas's Hospital in London discovered that by looking through coloured glass screens he could see a definite band of light, six inches wide emanating from the body. He further discovered that the band of light changed shape and colour depending on the health of the subject and realized its immense potential for diagnostic purposes.

Inventing a glass screen which hermetically sealed solutions of dycyanin dyes, he was able to perceive a misty light around the head and shoulders and hands of his human guinea pigs when he stood them up against a black back drop.

In his book *The Aura*, he describes the luminosity appearing in three layers, the innermost of which he refers to as 'the etheric double', the middle as the 'inner aura', surrounded by the 'outer aura'.

The whole aura, he found, was sensitive to magnetism and electric current which, when applied, vanished to reappear again with greater intensity.

Not everyone was able to see Kilner's auras, though using his screens, and he explained that he had had to spend a good deal of time before carrying out his experiments getting his eyes accustomed to looking through his screen by first staring at daylight through darker glass. He also claimed that he was perhaps more sensitive to auras than others, and that this is likely is explained in this passage from Lyall Watson's *Supernature*:

> Our eyes are sensitive to light that lies between the wavelengths of 380 and 760 millimicrons. With very high intensity artificial sources we can extend this at either end of the spectrum into the areas of infrared and ultraviolet light. The fact that man's body sends out electro-magnetic waves just too long for most people to see has been vividly demonstrated by the new 'thermographic' technique, which translates heat radiation into wonderful colour pictures. Atoms generate infrared rays by their constant motion, and the warmer they are the more active they become. In thermographic portraits, cold hair and fingernails show up black or blue, cool earlobes are green, the nose is a lukewarm yellow, and the neck and cheeks glow with orange and red. The system is now being used to detect tumours, arthritis, and cancer, which show up as isolated hot areas.

Note: Shampoo advertisements on television demonstrate thermographic hair as an easily accessible example.

> So the body does radiate on a wavelength just outside our normal vision, and this radiation changes according to the health of the transmitter.
>
> Perhaps Kilner was right. The range of human sensitivity is quite wide: some people hear sounds that to others are supersonic, and some people see wavelengths that to others are invisible. Those who claim to be able to see an aura surrounding living things could be supersensitive at the infrared end of the spectrum. Waves this length are beyond the capability of the cone-shaped cells in our retina, which appreciate visible colours, but they may be within the range of the rod-shaped cells that are more sensitive to low light intensities.

Kilner's theories and discoveries had to wait till 1939 before they gained credibility among the scientific factions. In Krasnador, southern Russia, near the Black Sea, lived an electrician, Semyon Kirlian. He was an extremely competent man and his services were often called upon by researchers working at the local hospital to repair the various pieces of equipment when they malfunctioned.

One day, while in a laboratory, Kirlian was present during a demonstration of a new high frequency electrotherapy unit.

As the patient received the treatment through electrodes, Kirlian noticed minute flashes of light sparking between the person's skin and the electrodes themselves.

An amateur photographer, fascinated by the infinite possibilities offered by the photographic plate, he wondered whether it would be possible to record these minute skin flashes.

He realized that since the electrodes were made of glass for safety, the photographic plate would be ruined by exposure to light before the unit could even be switched on, so he decided to use metal electrodes, though this was clearly dangerous.

Placing his own hand in the right position after adjusting the photographic plate, he switched on the power, was instantly and painfully burnt, but hoped that after the three seconds he had exposed the plates, he might have an original photograph.

When the plate was developed he saw a very strange imprint. Around the contours of his fingers a luminosity had been recorded.

He set to work developing a machine that would photograph this apparent aura. The known techniques of photography without light – X-Ray and infrared – he knew would be of no use, so he devised a process that would only catch this new luminous energy emanating from the body.

Helped by his wife, Valentina, a journalist and teacher, he eventually found a method of taking the pictures he wanted and his first successful result was the photograph of a leaf revealing, around its edges, millions of light energy dots flaring in turquoise and orange patterns from the direction of the leaf's veins.

When he similarly photographed his own finger, it appeared on the picture like an erupting volcano, flames of energy sparking from the tips.

As these were static pictures, the husband and wife team went on to perfect an optical instrument that would enable them to see their discovery in motion and, according to the Ostrander and Schroeder report in *Psychic Discoveries Behind the Iron Curtain*:

> The hand itself looked like the Milky Way in a starry sky. Against a background of blue or gold, something was taking place in the hand that looked like a firework display. Multicoloured flares lit up, then sparks, twinkles, flashes. Some lights glowed steadily like Roman candles, others flashed out then dimmed. Still others sparked at intervals. In parts of his hand there were little dim clouds. Certain glittering flares meandering along sparkling labyrinths like spaceships travelling to other galaxies.
>
> When the Kirlians placed a fresh leaf under the lens of a microscope connected to the high frequency generator, they saw a picture similar to that of the human hand. Next they tried a half withered leaf. It looked like a great metropolis turning out its lights for the night. They tried an almost completely withered leaf. There were almost no flares and sparks and 'clouds' scarcely moved. As they watched, the leaf seemed to be dying before their eyes and its death was reflected in the picture of energy impulses. 'We appeared to be seeing the very life activities of the leaf itself,' Kirlian said, 'intense, dynamic energy in the healthy leaf, less in the withered leaf, nothing in the dead leaf.'

This Kirlian discovery soon made scientific news and, with the backing of the Soviet Academy of Sciences, they elaborated further on their machines and carried out endless experiments.

What they proved was what mediums had been saying for years, that living matter has an aura, and that that aura is affected by frequencies of energy governed by the state of health of the subject. Fatigue, poor states of mind, anxieties and illnesses all contribute to the behaviour of the aura.

When the Kirlians examined two leaves side by side taken from similar plants and saw a sharp contrast, they were puzzled. But a visiting scientist who had given them the leaves was quite ecstatic.

Both leaves were torn from the same species of plant, but one of these plants had already been contaminated with a serious plant disease. You've found this out immediately! There is absolutely nothing on the plant or this leaf to indicate that it has been infected and will soon die. No tests on the actual plant or the leaf show anything wrong with it. With high frequency photography you've diagnosed illness in the plant *ahead of time*!

In the Ostrander and Schroeder book a series of photographs are reproduced. These show, among other things, the changes in luminescence of a fingertip when the subject was calm and even tempered compared to the fingertip when the subject was in a state of fatigue. The aura, when the person is calm, resembles a glowing coal fire, when fatigued, like the exhaust of flaring rockets.

Psychics who can see auras all seem to agree that the luminescence around the human body is egg-shaped, wide around the head and shoulders, tapering towards the feet.

In the famous book, *The Teachings of Don Juan: A Yaqui Way of Knowledge* by Carlos Castaneda, who wrote it when he was a graduate student at the University of California, this egg-shaped aura is briefly but interestingly mentioned.

In 1960, Carlos Castaneda first met Don Juan, a Yaqui Indian feared and shunned by the ordinary folk of the American South West because of his unnatural powers. During the next five years Don Juan's arcane knowledge led him into a world of beauty and terror, ruled by concepts far beyond those of Western civilization. Using psychedelic drugs – peyote, jimson weed and mushroom humito – Castenada lived through encounters with disembodied spirits, shamans in the form of huge wolves, and death in the shape of silver crows. Three times he met Mescalito, the god of peyote; finally, after a night of terror in which he realized his life was threatened by forces which he still cannot fully explain, he gave up the struggle to become a Man of Knowledge – to find the other you – but wrote his remarkable book in which Don Juan tells him:

I like to sit in parks and bus depots and watch. Real people look like luminous eggs when you *see* them. In a crowd of egglike creatures you can spot the one who looks just like a person, then you know that there is something wrong and that, without this luminous glow, this is not a real person at all.

Having accepted that all living matter is surrounded by a field of force which can sometimes be seen or photographed as an aura, there is also the aura which is perceived by psychics that differs slightly in that it is coloured by the thought processes of the subject.

This colouring ranges from fine violet, blue hues to yellows, dark browns, greys and dull reds. Sometimes the auras shine with a pure golden light, which, if some of the interpretations put on colour can be proved to be correct, signifies spirituality.

Pale blues and purples are interpreted as the given power of healing.

Pink for pure love and affection.

Red for desire and anger.

Green for intellect.

Browns and muddy shades going to greys signify disease.

An aura which appears to be shrivelling suggests approaching death.

These colours, however, are not always reliable symbols and should not be applied as hard and fast rules. What matters most in the aura is its clarity and purity of colours which indicates stability, or instability in the subject's character. Blues merging into reds merging into greys like a dirty artist's palate is suspect. A clear yellow outlined by a pure green is obviously more sound.

The acquisition of auric sight, like all other paranormal faculties, is a question of practice and patience. Compared to other forms of psychic powers it is, however, relatively simple to try out, providing you give yourself time and do not limit yourself to only one or two experiments.

Auric sight is one of the faculties which may indicate that you can develop other powers in the psychic field, but apart from this, and possibly confirming that a person is physically or mentally unwell because of the poor state of their aura, auric sight can only be regarded as a fascinating additional and supernatural dimension. Even if you are as developed as Eileen Garrett and can actually walk down a street seeing people around you surrounded by their egg-shaped multicoloured screens, it will tell you little about them except how they feel. Useful, perhaps, when visiting a bank manager to ask for a loan – if he has a glowing red aura, then it may be best to leave the meeting to another day, or if yours is grey and dull brown, maybe you are not giving off as confident a vibration of character as is suitable for the occasion.

TESTING YOUR AURA

Before setting out to look at other people's auras, it is a good idea to try a sample test or two on yourself.

Against a dark background, with not too much light behind you, extend your arms and hands, then turn both hands inwards so that the fingers of the right hand are pointing at the fingers of the left hand, palms facing you.

Focus six inches or so *beyond* your hands, then bring your eyes in to focus on the tips of your fingers.

Gradually you will see a vague grey shadow around the finger tips, then a misty line extending from one finger tip to the other.

To make sure that this is not an optical illusion, drop one hand six inches or so and the misty grey extension of your fingers should curve, still remaining as a bridge between the hands.

The grey luminosity will be extremely faint, but it will be there, and it will seem so normal that you will not in fact believe your eyes. This will be your first sight of your own aura, and you are probably ready to experiment further.

I have found, when checking my aura with this hand experiment, that television light helps a great deal. Situating yourself in a dark room with your back to the television set and facing a dark wall, you will be able to see your finger aura after a very short

136

time if you turn the television itself to the wall and switch it on so that it gives a constant blue-grey light reflected off that wall.

Similarly, a northern evening light coming through a gauzed window provides ideal conditions.

Once you are satisfied that you know what the aura looks like, you should now be moving on to trying to see someone else's, and for this you of course need a willing subject.

The person, male or female, should stand against a dark background – dark blue, green or deep red velvet drapes are preferable, with, if possible, the northern evening light, or television reflection coming from an area in front of them.

The subject should be nude, facing you or with their back to you, and you yourself should sit in a relaxed position to gaze, not stare, at the subject.

You should, as with your hand experiment, focus your eyes a foot or so *beyond* the subject, losing your vision in the depths of the dark background, then slowly bring the eyes to focus on and around the person. At this point you should see a very very faint misty grey light around the outline of the body. *However*, if you have inadvertently begun to stare, and your eyes are suffering from optical fatigue, you may see more than you've bargained for. Very exciting flames of yellow or gold will seem to emanate from the person before you, but this will only be an illusion. You have forced a result on the session and your eyes have begun to see stars.

If this happens, stop, relax for at least ten minutes by going into another room or looking out of the window at something in the far distance.

When you are ready to start again, do so when you are quite relaxed, and when you eventually manage to achieve an auric sighting of the grey mist, check that this is not an optical illusion by looking right round the contours of the subject. The mist may have breaks in it, it may have bulges, but if there is a continuity, then you have probably got the person's aura in your sights. Ask them to turn round slowly so that you see them in profile, and again check round the contours of their body for the faint grey mist. Ask them to face you again and lift one arm, and you should see the aura between the under arm and the hip where the mist will be at its widest. It is in this area that you will eventually be able to discern colours – but not for a while.

What you have to do now, *once you have got this far*, is to accustom your eyes to spotting the aura, and this, it must be emphasized, like everything else in psychic development, *takes time*.

When you are able to switch on your auric sight at will in the special conditions you have created with the dark backdrop and/ or television light, you should try and see people's auras in normal everyday conditions. Dark corners of railway stations or in the Underground is obviously a good place to start. The audience sitting in a cinema can sometimes lend itself to good auric atmosphere, but if a film is showing the light intensity changes so frequently that it can prove a total waste of time, besides which, you should be looking at the faces of the audience, not an audience that is between you and the screen. A fully developed psychic can, for instance, see multiple auras when walking up the aisle from the screen to the exit doors at the back, provided the light coming from the screen is fairly constant.

If your family are patient with you, you can see multiple auras when you sit next to your television screen while they are watching a programme. Chat shows tend to have constant light, and if they allow you to turn the colour to black and white, all the better.

But here I am talking of a fully developed person who may have proved himself sufficiently adept at seeing auras to have been able to convince his friends and relations that he will be able to tell them how they are within themselves.

Like Kilner's auric coloured plates, your eyes should be able to discern anyone who is feeling below par, but maybe has not admitted it. You may also be able to spot a serious illness – but here you should obviously tread carefully before voicing your

138

non medical opinion. Some people are very vulnerable to autosuggestion.

As mentioned before, a clear, pure, aura is a good sign, a misty, 'dirty' aura suggests sickness. This may not be only indicative of health, but of vitality. The aura mirrors one's vitality, indeed it may be the one visible sign of one's vitality. There is a theory that a break in a person's aura, like a wound, is an indication that their life force has been escaping, has been drawn out by a greater force, or actually sucked out by another person's more powerful personality.

That in everyday life we meet people who by their sheer zest for living draw one's energy, leaving one depleted, is a fact, and this type of 'leakage of energy' shows up in what is known by psychics as 'aura tears', and should one of your subjects have many of these, it is likely that they will be very subdued with little will of their own.

They can be helped.

Auras, that is vitality, can be recharged, just as one's energy is recharged by eating the right kinds of food.

Just as vegetables provide us with certain vitamins, vegetation can also provide us with auric vitality. Some plants 'suck' at our auras, others have a surplus of vitality and can recharge us. Trees, it is said, are great boosters, and pine trees and fir trees are the best. If you feel devitalized, try sitting at the foot of a tree with your back firmly against the base of the trunk and think yourself into being 'as one' with that tree. Minou Drouet, a nine year old poet prodigy in the 1950s, made headlines by writing a sonnet entitled 'Arbre Mon Ami'. That is what you should convey to the tree, that it is your friend, that you like it, love it and that it loves you back. Relax as much as you can while pressing your back against the tree and thinking yourself into these thoughts. After fifteen minutes or so, you will feel the difference.

Needless to say that the above suggestion can be easily written off as 'daft', but if you are honest with yourself you will admit that you often have some affection for certain trees or plants.

139

Don't ignore this feeling, do not regard it as fantasy from cloud cuckoo land; something is going on between you and that plant and tree and both can benefit. Sit against it, or as near to it as possible, and see if you can get any energy from it.

If pines or firs are not easily accessible, beeches, oaks and apple trees are a good second best. Elms, according to one psychic, should be avoided. Long before they started dying of Dutch Elm disease, they were regarded by those in the know as negative powers.

In my own various experiments in trying to see the aura I have managed on several occasions to get a colour glow round my own hand, but have not, so far, achieved instant or even controlled auric sight outside what I would call my 'laboratory'. I will, however, mention how I got as far as I did, stressing immediately that I believe my poor eyesight may have helped to contribute to the success.

I am myopic, short sighted to a boring degree, and tend to be colour blind on greens and blues when the shades get close to turquoise. I wear spectacles from morn to night and, this may be very important, have taken to using photochromatic lenses for some time. These are the lenses which, like magic, get darker or lighter depending on the intensity of light.

One summer's Sunday when I was on the balcony of my apartment reading the newspaper and the sun was shining brightly, my spectacles were reacting correctly by darkening and allowing me comfortable vision. I was intrigued by a recipe in one of the colour supplements and, as the lunch hour was approaching, I decided to have a go at cooking.

The all important earthenware casserole was kept in the oven, and when I went into the comparatively darker kitchen, my spectacles cleared slowly. I crouched down, opened the oven door and reached inside for the casserole. As I did so I perceived a glow around my hands which was at first quite frightening. It was a topaz haze and moved just like a haze does on hot asphalt roads. When I held up my hand as I might to examine my fingernails, it was as though I were wearing large transparent gloves of a light brown hue.

I had two instant thoughts.

One, that some psychic message was coming through from my subconscious warning me that I might burn my hands while cooking this dish unless I wore oven gloves. The second was that I was staring at my own aura.

As my spectacles lightened and became totally clear, the aura disappeared.

I did not come to the conclusion that my lenses played a part in this auric vision till the next day, though I tried unsuccessfully to repeat the experiment several times that Sunday – totally forgetting about the recipe, of course.

When I then moved quickly from bright sunlight to a darker kitchen and thrust my hands in the even blacker oven, I twice more got the auric vision.

For reasons I cannot explain, other than that it was as much to do with my own mood, or health at the time, or it was something to do with the weather, I was never able again to achieve such a sighting. All that I was able to conclude from the incident was that my aura was a not very clear, not a very pure brown which suggested that, at the time anyway, I was unwell. In fact, two days later, according to my diary, I went down with a heavy summer cold.

For those who try in vain to get auric sightings but fail, there is an alternative – that of auric touch.

It is a very subtle and not too easy way of coming into contact with another person's aura, and one that you cannot try on yourself with any satisfactory degree of success.

Ask your subject either to sit up in a chair, or lie down on a bed or on the ground and remain quite still. Pass your hands over their body, keeping them two or three inches above the skin surface.

Move your hands downwards from head to feet slowly, as though you were in fact feeling the surface of the aura itself, and concentrate hard on what reactions the tips of your fingers are getting, willing them to feel something.

Lift your hands six to eight inches above this imagined aura as you go over the body again, then bring them down close to within two or three inches of the surface as you did before.

By repeating this exercise many times you should eventually feel a difference in the air texture, a warmth or an unexpected coolness in certain areas. Go over these different areas comparing them to other sensations and, closing your eyes, you will get a picture through your finger tips of the shape of the aura that is enveloping your subject.

As the experiment can take an extremely long time and it is unusual to be able to get the co-operation of a subject with as much patience as you will need, try auric touch while the subject is asleep.

A sleeping child is an extremely good subject as their bodies are so small and compact and their auras are usually tighter round their tiny frames.

I spent a four hour session passing my hands over my five-year-old daughter's sleeping form one night, with rather satisfactory results.

I definitely felt changes in temperature about three inches above and around her head and shoulders and, strangely, around her knees, losing any sense of touch over her chest and small stomach. The feet were very peculiar, as though the aura was cone shaped to a height of some nine inches above the tips of her toes. I was not sure enough about this that first night, and on subsequent nights could not get anything at all, but I did learn that the 'cone' night had followed on a day when she had seen a tap dancing programme on television and had decided to become a tap dancer, not stopping for a second from the time the programme ended till she went to bed – tapping!

A psychic warmth then over exercised little feet, or autosuggestive dreams of ambition to compete with Gene Kelly and Tommy Tune?

Auric touch is not as satisfactory as auric vision, but it does lead straight to another important supernatural force, that of faith healing.

10
FAITH HEALING

I will have conveyed by now that I am not a man who has any great religious beliefs. I am able to put aside Christianity without a feeling of guilt, and read with great interest but no particular rapport the teachings of Buddha, Calvin, the Bhagavad-gita, the Upanishads or Mohammed. When it comes to having faith in the potential of people's psychic powers, however, I embrace the idea willingly, which is perhaps why I was cured very quickly of an attack of shingles, a few years back, which threatened to spread across my face and affect my eyes.

I was in Spain at the time and had seen a number of doctors who told me that I would just have to put up with the extreme discomfort and hope that the unpleasant rash would not advance upwards. Shingles is a nervous disease which one can do little about, there is no medical treatment and no lotion that one can put on that does anything but alleviate the pain.

When a friend suggested I should visit the local witch who miraculously cured rashes, I did not hesitate, open minded as always and naturally fascinated at the prospect of meeting a real live sorceress, cauldron, broomstick and all.

The witch turned out to be a pleasantly plump lady in her

sixties with neat hairdresser's blue rinse and sporting a floral patterned frock. She examined me from a distance, then sat me down in front of her and, as though feeling for my aura, passed her hands over my head and shoulders and round the back of my neck where the shingles was at its worst. She then gently slapped the affected parts of my skin with a tiny brush made of marjoram twigs (as near to a broomstick as I got) and that was that.

She charged 'whatever I wanted to give' which she apparently passed on to charity, and I left feeling none the better but none the worse.

Three days later the shingle rash started to disappear, within a week it was over.

Shingles usually lasts at least a month, often very much longer.

The witch was a faith healer; *my* faith in her, *her* faith in her own powers.

And that is where the secret lies in faith healing. If you have any doubts at all in the power of the person who claims they can heal you, it is more than likely that they will fail.

The majority of doctors, while remaining sceptical about the origins and extent of the faith healer's powers, admit that such healing very often benefits a patient when the disease is 'hysterical'. If the more sensible ones baulk at the mention of faith healers, it is not that they regard it as black magic lunacy, but fear that some patients may seek such an unorthodox method of cure *before* consulting them and knowing what they are actually suffering from.

A medical encyclopedia describes faith healing in the following terms:

The belief and practice of curing physical and mental ills by faith in some supernatural power, either allegedly latent in the individual (as with Christian Science) or drawn in some way from God. It is a characteristic of faith healing that it is supposed to be publicly demonstrable – i.e. – a 'healer' will hold public meetings and invite sick people to come up to be cured on the platform. In the emotionally charged atmosphere which the healer generates, it is not unusual for people to show immediate and striking improvement in their illness,

145

but the almost invariable rule is for relapses to occur within days or hours of the event. When remission is more permanent, the illness is generally hysterical in origin and will often return to the individual in some other form. Spiritualists claim that the healing in such cases is not done by 'faith' but by direct intervention of the spirits of doctors etc., who have died and passed on to another world.

Though my own shingles were hysterical in origin, I do not remember suffering any other form of setback, nor do I believe for one moment that my particular 'witch' believed she was working through the help of doctors departed. Spain being a Roman Catholic country, it is more likely that she simply believed she had a gift from God, which was enough for her to trust her own powers, and I, as mentioned before, was ready to believe in her.

Faith healing, of course, goes back in history as far as the cave medicine man. Jesus Christ was obviously the most notable faith healer of all time, but its practice gathered momentum in the middle ages, waned a little for a time then suffered a major setback due to the plagues against which faith healers proved to have no power.

Medicine came to be administered by physicians and the use of surgery and bone setting became accepted as the norm; faith healers slipped further into the province of the less respected, along with witches, wizards and astrologers.

An Irishman, however, revived the interest in faith healing by impressing the chemist Robert Boyle (1627-1691). He demonstrated that he could draw diseases out of sick persons, attributing his power to God.

Faith healing, based on religious fervour, grew apace again from then on, and was given a boost in the mid-eighteenth century by an Austrian priest, Johann Gassner, who used dramatic exorcism techniques to cure his patients, sending them into frightening trances which produced convulsions and comas. The Church did not look upon his activities with too much pleasure and requested him to desist.

Anton Mesmer came on the scene as a faith healer at this time, and cured his patients in groups, requesting them to hold the ends of iron rods which were planted in a bed of iron filings. Sending them into a trance – mesmerising them – they came out of the experience feeling better.

Mesmer did not see himself as a faith healer, but as a scientist. He believed that the universe surrounded us with a power which could be tapped and transferred into 'animal magnetism', and that this magnetism was essential to good health. Those who failed to draw enough of this power into themselves by natural means fell ill and, by using his methods, could recharge the power, like batteries, and become well again.

It was all a question of faith, and though his ideas were adopted by others, they were gradually changed to suit more fashionable beliefs.

An American healer, Phineas Quimby, who used Mesmer's methods, gained the reputation of being more of a clairvoyant than a Mesmerist, and though Mary Baker Eddy (1821-1910), the founder of Christian Science, started her career as a faith healer similarly using Mesmerism as the basis for her cures, she jettisoned his trance and hypnotism techniques in favour of making her patients believe that her curing powers came direct from God. All that she asked of her followers was to have faith in God and in the omnipresence of his Divine Mind, and her method gained rapid popularity.

The Church started to play a more important part in the faith healing movement from then on, at least in people's minds. Faith healers with reputations of success were idolized and found themselves being placed on similar pedestals to Jesus Christ himself. Congregations flocked to see them heal the sick, and faith healing became associated totally with Christianity, though the Church itself made no move to support them. It was pleased, however, to get the credit for miraculous cures; the Roman Catholic church especially mounted the band wagon of miracle healing, promoting such saintly places as Lourdes, in South West

147

France, to an unacceptable degree of commercialism as far as genuine healers were concerned.

The main argument that crops up whenever the subject of faith healing is raised is that faith healing is nothing more than suggestion.

Call it faith-in-the-suggestion-of-healing if it is preferable, I doubt whether it matters very much if the person who believes they are going to be cured, *is* cured.

Dr H.J. Eynsenck, Professor of the Psychology Department in the University of London, Director of Psychological Department at the Institute of Psychiatry as well as Visiting Professor at the Universities of Pennsylvania and California, has written on *suggestion* in his book *Uses and Abuses of Psychology*:

'We cannot,' he writes, 'be said to understand at all well the way in which suggestion works, but there is ample factual evidence to leave us in no doubt about its potential power.'

He describes a typical experiment carried out on children to find out the power of suggestion in the getting rid of warts compared to the use of orthodox medical treatment.

Two groups of children with warts were put under observation Group A received ordinary medical care, while Group B were daily shown a picture of a wart, the wart becoming smaller and smaller every day in the new pictures till the last drawing showed no wart at all.

Group B lost their warts more quickly than medically treated Group A proving that the response to suggestion was a power to be considered seriously.

This experiment was carried out on children who were aware of what was happening, but Dr Eysenck goes on to say that it is not necessary for suggestion to be conscious to be effective, and he cites another experiment on children suffering from the bad habit of nail-biting.

Again, the children were separated into two groups, A and B, each group having its own dormitory.

Over a period of one month Group A was allowed to sleep

undisturbed, but Group B was subjected to a soft voice broadcast over a gentle sound system which repeated endlessly, once all the children were asleep. . .'I will not bite my finger nails. Finger nail biting is a dirty habit. I will never bite my finger nails again.' Before any of the children were likely to wake up, the voice was switched off.

None of the children in Group B were ever aware that a record had been played to them during the thirty odd nights of the experiment, but more of them than in Group A stopped biting their nails in the weeks that followed.

My personal interest in faith healing is not so much what the healers time and time again manage to do, but the quite incredibly high wall of official scepticism that is built round any one of them who nowadays appears to prove his powers.

In the *Encyclopedia of the Unexplained*, two cases are mentioned in the short section on faith healing which I reproduce below. As far as paranormal activities are concerned, it is clear that we are progressing with one step forward at a time, and regressing with two steps backwards immediately afterwards.

A project was recently put forward for a scientific test of *Absent Healing*, where individual healers, or groups of their followers, pray for the sick. The idea was to take a hospital ward, and divide its members into two groups: half of them would be prayed for and the other half left as controls. If such a test failed, it could of course be attributed to the inability of those praying to rouse the vital force under test conditions. But if it succeeded, it would be quite a convincing demonstration of the power of absent healing – so long as suitable precautions were taken to prevent either the patients, or their doctors and nurses, from knowing which patients were in which group. But the project had to be abandoned when the hospital authorities pointed out that *if* the experiment worked, it would mean that the patients who had responded were being treated by unqualified practitioners. This would be contrary to regulations of the General Medical Council; any doctor who had co-operated would find himself liable to be erased from the medical register.

It ought to be possible, in some instances, to demonstrate the existence of faith healing by its results in individual cases. Many attempts have been made to do so, notably with patients who have been told they have cancer, and who have biopsy results to prove it, but who then after going to a healer are found to have no trace of cancer. There are several such cases, well attested. Confronted with them, however, the medical profession has resorted to defensive rationalizations. The biopsy (it is claimed) must have been taken from somebody else by mistake; or, in taking the fragment of the patient for the biopsy, all cancer was luckily removed too; or, it must have been a case of spontaneous regression, nothing to do with the healer.

This section fortunately ends with a happier note where healing on enzyme activity and on metabolism is being researched, not in the UK, of course, but in the USA where they are obviously more broad minded.

THE GIFT OF HEALING
Faith healing, unlike other forms of psychic abilities, cannot be acquired by study or practice. It is a *gift*. If the gift of composing music, painting a masterpiece or writing a trenchant piece of poetry is a gift of God, then faith healing has a right to be linked with religious faith.

All this is to point out that there is no method by which you can become a healer – you either are or are not – what you have to do, however, is find out whether you have this gift.

There are stories of how certain people who had no thoughts about faith healing discovered that they had this power, usually when going to a healer themselves in desperation following the failure of ordinary medicine. One story I particularly like, though, is that of a friend of mine, a young television documentary director who, when setting up a programme on *The Unexplained*, interviewed a faith healer who very quickly told him, 'But you have this power yourself'. It apparently takes one healer to recognize another, but you can also make a few tentative experiments yourself. To do so there is no better way than going through the auric touch tests mentioned in the previous chapter with a subject suffering from some painful malaise to see if you can cure them.

Many faith healers, you should be warned, who draw the sickness from a patient, take it into themselves.

Those who relieve a subject from a bad headache, for example, often find that they have the headache afterwards, usually to a quite unbearable degree.

A sure sign that you are a healer is the heat which your hands will generate, as though you had a high temperature. It is a heat that the patients themselves will also feel.

Those well practised in healing have various ways of protecting themselves from catching the diseases they draw from the sufferers, but it is really beyond the scope of this book to go into that on a practical level – and should you sense at all that you might have a certain power, then seek out a healer and ask his advice.

Faith healing is one area of supernatural power where the other you can really help your fellow men.

Suggested further reading:
Health, Radiation and Healing. M. Ash. Darton, Longman & Todd.
Faith Healing. L. Rose. Gollancz.
The Nature of Healing. A Guirdham. Allen & Unwin.

11
ASTRAL PROJECTION

FACT IS STRANGER THAN FICTION
Extract from fiction:

She was breathing heavily, regularly, fast asleep beside him when the telephone rang.

'Hello? Who is that?'

'It's me. Melanie.'

'What do you mean, Melanie?'

'It's *me* Michael, Melanie.'

He held onto the receiver, sat up and shook Melanie right next to him. Her body was quite cold. Ice cold. He looked at her, the skin was so pale it was nearly translucent.

'Astral projection Michael. I'm not with you in bed, I'm back here in France, in your home.'

It was her voice, some sort of ventriloquist trick.

He shook the body next to him.

'Who are you really?' He was frightened.

'I've travelled through space, Michael. Astral projection. You don't believe me, do you? Just put the receiver down and ring me back.'

He put the receiver down slowly, then slipped out of the bed. Somehow Melanie's inert body cold, pale, made him feel uneasy.

How could she be speaking to him from France when she was right here in New York?

Slowly he drew off the blanket, the top sheet, and stared at her. She was quite white. He switched on the centre light. It was like looking at a marble sculpture.

He touched her. The flesh was hard, bloodless, the lips white, her eyes tight shut, the fists clenched. She was doubled up in the foetus position, as though cringing from an impact.

He slipped his hands under her, turned her over. There were bruises on her shoulders, bruises and scratches down her back; it was as though she had been through a hailstorm, or a triplex window.

He reached out for the telephone and dialled the French number.

'Hi!' Melanie's voice said.

'Just explain to me how you do it.'

'Mind over matter,' she said simply. 'Anyone can do it if they work on themselves. I'm going to come back now. You can watch if you want to, but it might put you off me, I understand one goes into spasms and convulsions. . .see you.'

Premonitions of an Inherited Mind

Factual extract

I did some window browsing at Hammacher-Schlemmer's and then looked at my watch. I saw that it was nearly 6.00. I had to get back to the apartment to change, then get to the Biltmore. I often jog when I'm going places in New York, for the exercise, and since I didn't want to be late I started jogging about a block away from the apartment, which was east of Second Avenue and almost to First Avenue. It was now just a few minutes past 6.00 p.m.

Andrija was out at his home in Ossining, more than 30 miles away and about an hour away from Manhattan from door to door, either by train or by car – sometimes longer during the rush hour.

So, a very few minutes after 6.00 I was starting to jog about a block away from the apartment. Andrija was watching TV in Ossining (he told me later) more than an hour away.

I clearly remember approaching the canopy of the building right next to ours. I remember almost reaching that canopy. Then I remember having that feeling that I was running backward for a couple of steps. I don't know whether I really did or not, but that was the feeling. Then I had the feeling that I was being sucked upward. There was no sensation in my body. I closed my eyes and, I think, opened them almost immediately.

When I did, I found myself being propelled in the air a foot or so away from a porch screen, over the top of a rhododendron bush, about to crash through a screen at a point 8 to 10 feet off the ground. To prepare for the impact, I turned my left shoulder toward the screen and put my hands out in front of me. I crashed through the screen and landed on a circular glass top table. It was heavy plate glass. My hands hit it first, and it slid forward, then hit the floor and shattered. My knee struck a wooden part of the table, and the table toppled over. I landed on the floor of the porch. I was conscious all through this, but slightly dazed when I hit the table and floor. My knee hurt and I was frightened to move in case I had any broken bones. But what shocked me was that I recognized the porch and the table because I knew them so well. This was Andrija's screen porch in Ossining – there was no mistaking it. One moment I had been on the East side of Manhattan. The next I was crashing through the screen and hitting the table and floor. I called out loud as I could to Andrija, but there was no answer right away. I remember being cold and very thirsty. I still was afraid to move.

Andrija added more for me later. He had watched just about half of the six o'clock news. About 6.15 p.m. he heard a crash, followed by a thud, as if something hit the side of the house. Since it was a windy evening he thought perhaps a tree had toppled against the house. He went out of the front door to the porch. Although he couldn't see anything he heard me calling. He went back into the house and through the dining room and into the study. He threw on the light switch and opened the door to the porch. He told me that he saw me lying in a heap beside the broken glass and table, and then looked up and saw a huge gaping hole in the screen, which was pushed in from the top above his head level. He saw that I was holding a package, which contained binoculars I had just bought in New York.

My Story, Uri Geller.

Astral projection turns the potential psychic into Superman.

It takes years of hard work, of concentration, of practice and patience, but it can be done – has been done.

The whole subject of astral projection is so fraught with improbabilities that you must, from the outset, understand fully that any of us leave our minds, leave our bodies on many occasions without being aware of it.

Claims by a person that they have projected themselves to another place on earth or into an unknown area altogether – an astral plane – can always be disregarded as vivid imagination, a dream or lunacy, but there are imagined or dream like moments throughout one's life that we remember for ever, from which we do not recover, so extraordinary they have been, and it is one of

154

these experiences which should be recalled, dissected and analysed.

As an example of what I mean I will recount a moment in time when I was fourteen which I believe was such an extraordinary experience, when, perhaps, I projected myself onto another plane, but which I disregarded as a 'strange dream' for the twenty odd years or so that followed because it never occurred to me that it might have been psychic.

I was at my boarding school, sick and in the sanatorium probably delirious with fever.

In the small ward with me was another boy, Harris, suffering from the same infection. We were, therefore, both ill, more than likely being given the same drugs and in an ideal state to 'see things'.

In the middle of the night (or was it the day?) I got out of bed, drawn to the window by a particularly bright light and a feeling that there was something to be seen. I opened the window and looked out onto what might best be described as a child's idea of heaven, that is an exceptionally beautiful garden of yellows and pink, green and blue pastel shades and the feeling, I remember the feeling to this day, that all was well, all was really very well, that I need fear nothing ever any more, here was true comfort and security and love and everything else that one could wish oneself. As I stood by the window I was joined by Harris, who snivelled, and he looked out of the window at the same scene with amazement but with much more acceptance than I. He smiled with satisfaction and signalled me to return to bed in case matron came, conveying, 'It's there, we know it's there, we've plenty of time yet.'

Presumably I went back to bed and dropped off to sleep, for I awoke later and sat up remembering the experience. It was a dream, I thought, how could it have been anything else, the window, right there, looked out onto a redbrick forecourt, but it was so vivid that I started recounting everything to Harris.

He paled, and said that he had had exactly the same dream, that

155

he had joined me by the window but that *I* had told *him*, without speaking, that we should go back to bed, that we had plenty of time, that we knew it was there and no longer had to worry.

Harris, brighter than myself, worried the experience for quite a time, deciding that it was a precognition of our joint deaths because we were suffering from an incurable undiagnosed disease. In fact I was discharged two days later, and he the day after that and the incident was forgotten.

But was it just a clairvoyant vision of heaven, or a sudden sighting of an astral plane?

Like travelling clairvoyance, astral projection appears to the unprepared to be so much of an imagined experience or a dream that it is only when you have worked very hard on yourself and *expect* to see something unimaginable, that you can accept the fact that you are achieving a psychic experience.

You are the only one who can judge whether you are clairvoyant or reaching into a world beyond the one you usually live in. However much you explain to others what your experience means to you, how certain you are that you have travelled into another world or another dimension of time, *you* will be the only one who will be certain because it is a *gut* feeling, much more than intuition, much more than a premonition, much more than a dream because it becomes memorable – and the *memory* of such a psychic experience may be the only proof you will ever have that you have been through it.

But, so what?

So, memories are dangerous.

Luis Bunuel, the Spanish film director, writes in his memoirs – 'Our imagination, and our dreams, are forever invading our memories; and since we are all apt to believe in the reality of our fantasies, we end up transforming our lies into truths. Of course, fantasy and reality are equally personal, and equally felt, so their confusion is a matter of only relative importance.'

But is it confusion?

On very many occasions it is not.

For yourself you need have no fear of being able to tell the difference between fantasy and reality.

For the sceptics, let them think that you are confused, their opinion is really of no importance at all.

Physical upset or emotional setbacks are usually responsible for triggering off an unexpected psychic experience such as a clairvoyant sighting or an astral projection.

A similar occurrence to that which Harris and I experienced in our school sanatorium appears in Colin Wilson's *Occult* concerning a Mr Oliver Fox who, in 1902, developed a capacity for leaving his body.

'Fox had a dream, during the course of which it struck him suddenly that he must be dreaming. He went on dreaming; but the knowledge that this was only a dream produced a feeling of great clarity, and the scenery of the dream became unusually vivid and beautiful. He tried to develop this knack of self awareness in dreams: it happened infrequently, but when it did he always experienced the same feeling of clarity and beauty.

He also discovered that once he was 'in control' of the dream, he could float through brick walls, levitate and so on. What was happening was, in fact, the reverse of a nightmare, where your legs refuse to run. He gradually became fairly expert at inducing the dreams, but observed that if he tried to prolong them, he experienced a pain in his head. He assumed this to be the pineal gland, the unused 'eye' in the centre of the brain, which occult tradition declares to be the doorway to the 'other' state of your being (the other you). If he ignored the pain and continued the dream, the result was a feeling of 'bilocation', as if he had left his body and was floating above it, although still aware of his body.

Eventually he discovered that if he tried determinedly he could overcome the pain. When this happened, there was a kind of 'click' in his head – which he identified with the opening of the pineal door 'and he then felt himself to be wholly located in the scenery of his dream, which, as before, would appear far more beautiful than normal. These dreams were followed by a return to his body, and another dream to the effect that he was back in bed and waking up.'

In his book *Legends*, August Strindberg (1849-1912) the Swedish dramatist, recounts an involuntary astral projection following the domestic crisis which led to his separating from his second wife. It is so simple an experience, seemingly an imagined visit to his home, like any of us might make an imagined visit to anywhere, that one could shrug off as nothing too surprising – but the old lady mentioned (his mother in law in fact) *saw* him and wrote to him:

> I was passing through a dangerous illness in the French capital, when the longing to be in the bosom of my family overcame me to such a degree that I saw the inside of my house and for a moment forgot my surroundings, having lost the consciousness of where I was. I was really there behind the piano as I appeared, and the imagination of the old lady had nothing to do with the matter. But since she understood these kinds of apparitions, and knew their significance, she saw in it a precursor of death, and wrote to ask if I were ill.

Strindberg is not the only author to have experienced astral projection: Arnold Bennett, Emily Brönte, John Buchan, George Eliot, Ernest Hemingway, Arthur Koestler, D.H. Lawrence, George Meredith, William Wordsworth, make ten in all have all written about projection experiences.

Two more examples, however, are worth mentioning for their fascination. The first an amusing account of a somewhat mad series of projections by a seventeenth-century Italian monk, who became known as The Flying Monk, from Wilson's *Occult*.

> The feats of St Joseph of Copertino are well attested by many witnesses. Guiseppe Desa was born in Apulia, Italy, 1603, a strange sickly boy who became known as 'Open Mouth' because his mouth usually hung open; one commentator remarks that 'he was not far from what today we should call a state of feeble mindedness; a bishop described him as *idiota* (although the word meant innocent rather than idiotic). He was subject to 'ecstacies' and, even as a teenager, given to ascetic self torments that undermined his health. At the age of seventeen he was accepted into the Capuchin order, but dismissed

eight months later because of total inability to concentrate. Not long after, the order of Conventuals near Copertino accepted him as a stable boy, and at twenty two he became a Franciscan priest. He continued to starve and flagellate himself, acquiring a reputation for holiness. Then one day, in the midst of his prayers after mass, he floated off the ground and landed on the altar in a state of ecstacy. He was unburned by candle flames, and flew back to his previous place.

Sent to see the Pope, he was again seized by such rapture that he rose in the air. His flying fits seem to have been always associated with the state that the Hindus called *Samadhi*, ecstacy. His levitations ceased for two years when a hostile superior went out of his way to humiliate and persecute him; but after a holiday in Rome as a guest of the superior of the order, and an enthusiastic reception by the people of Assisi, he regained his good spirits and sailed fifteen yards to embrace the image of the Virgin on the altar.

He seems to have been a curious but simple case; floating in the air when in a state of delight seems to have been his sole accomplishment. The ecstacy did not have to be religious; on one occasion when shepherds were playing their pipes in church on Christmas Eve, he began to dance for sheer joy, then flew onto the high altar, without knocking over any of the burning candles. On another occasion, when he had flown past lamps and ornaments that blocked his way to the altar, his superior called him back, and he flew back to the place he had vacated. When a fellow monk remarked on the beauty of the sky, he shrieked and flew to the top of a nearby tree. He was also able to lift heavy weights; one story tells of how he raised a wooden cross that ten workmen were struggling to place in position, and flew with it to the hole that had been prepared for it. He was also able to make others float; he cured a demented nobleman by seizing his hair and flying into the air with him, remaining there a quarter of an hour, according to his biographer; he also seized the hand of a fellow priest and after dancing around with him, they both flew hand in hand. When on his death bed, at the age of sixty, the doctor in attendance observed, as he cauterized a septic leg, that Fr. Joseph was floating in the air six inches above the chair. He died saying he could hear the sounds and smell the scents of paradise.

The second example, a far more serious, more recent and well documented report of an out-of-body experience appears in Lyall Watson's *Romeo Error*.

A medical officer attached to the Royal Flying Corps crashed on take off at a small country airfield. He was thrown out of the cockpit, landed on his back and lay there showing no signs of consciousness. From the hollow in which the crash took place, none of the airfield buildings are visible, but the doctor apparently saw every stage of the rescue operation. He remembers looking down at the crash from the point of view of about two hundred feet above it and seeing his body lying near by. He saw his Brigadier and the uninjured pilot running towards the body, wondered why they were interested in it and wished they would let it alone. He saw the ambulance starting out of the hangar in which it was garaged and almost immediately stalling. He saw the driver get out, use a starting handle, run back to his seat, start off and then pause while a medical orderly jumped into the back. He watched the ambulance stop at a hospital hut where the orderly collected something and then continue on its way to the crash. The still unconscious doctor then had the feeling that he was travelling away from the airfield, over a nearby town, westwards across Cornwall and out at great speed over the Atlantic. The journey came to an end suddenly as he resumed consciousness to find the orderly pouring sal volatile down his throat. A later inquiry into the circumstances of the accident, proved that his view of the events on the airfield was correct in every detail.

GURDJIEFF'S VIEW OF ASTRAL PROJECTION

What then is the astral body? How can we project it voluntarily? In Gurdjieff's opinion, the clearest and most acceptable explanation that I have come across. . .

It is stated that all men have an 'astral body'. This is quite wrong. What may be called the 'astral body' is obtained by means of inner unity, that is, by means of terribly hard inner work and struggle. Man is not born with it. And only very few men acquire an 'astral body'. If it is formed it may continue to live after the death of the physical body, and it may be born again in another physical body. If it is not reborn, then, in the course of time, it also dies; it is not immortal but it can live long after the death of the physical body.

The astral body is not an indispensable implement for man. It is a great luxury which only a few can afford. A man can live quite well without an astral body. His physical body possesses all the functions necessary for life. A man without an astral body may even produce the impression of being a very intellectual or even spiritual man, and may deceive not only others but also himself.

160

Through his lectures and talks with P.D. Ouspensky, Gurdjieff elaborates on his theme of the astral body, explaining what it is, how it comes into being, but first one must understand two theoretic laws – the *law of three* and the *law of seven*, which he explains thus:

> The first fundamental law of the universe is the law of three forces, or three principles, or, as it is often called, the *law of three*. According to this law, every action, every phenomenon in all worlds without exception, is the result of a simultaneous action of three forces – the positive, the negative and the neutralizing.
>
> The next fundamental law of the universe is the *law of seven* or the *law of octaves*.

The universe consists of vibrations which come from every conceivable direction and proceed in every conceivable direction. They cross each other, collide, unite, strengthen, weaken, help each other on their way or stop the other's progress. They are continuous and proceed uninterruptedly, up or down, around and about, providing the impulse which gave them birth is not impeded or a resistance built up within the medium in which they proceed. When the impulse fails for some reason and the resistance within the medium strengthens, the vibrations behave differently and strange things can happen or can be made to happen. Generally, however, vibrations start somewhere, go happily on their haphazard way, which explains why there are no straight lines in nature, why unexplainable accidents occur and why everything with us is basically only thought, and things happen in a contrary way to that which we would prefer or even expect.

If a conscious effort is made, however, to impede the vibrations or change the impulse that powers them, new horizons can be viewed.

Gurdjieff compares this effort to the striking of a new note at the end of an octave, starting another scale of notes, or a cycle of events.

His explanation describes the similarity between the movement of vibrations to the musical octave do-re-mi-fa-so-la-ti and suggests that the rebirth of the octave cycle can be equivalent to a new life form.

As Gurdjieff's theories take four volumes of P.D. Ouspensky's work to expound I do not propose to summarize them here, but will simply ask you to accept that his 'octave' example is split up into 'note powers' enabling him to say this about the astral body's birth:

Hydrogen 'si 12' is the hydrogen which represents the final product of the transformation of food in the human organism. This is the matter with which sex works and which sex manufactures. It is 'seed' and 'fruit'.

Hydrogen 'si 12' can pass into 'do' (the next octave) with the help of an additional shock (effort, inner work). But this shock can be of a dual nature and different octaves can begin, one outside the organism which has produced 'si', and the other in the organism itself. The union of male and female 'si 12' and all that accompanies it constitutes the shock of the first kind and the new octave begun with its help develops independently as a new organism or a new life.

This is the normal and natural way to use the energy of 'si 12'. But in the same organism there is a further possibility. And this is the possibility of creating a new life within the actual organism, in which the 'si 12' has been manufactured, without the union of the two principles, the male and the female. A new octave then develops within the organism, not outside it. This is the birth of the astral body. You must understand that the astral body is born of the same material, of the same matter, as the physical body, only the process is different. The whole of the physical body, all its cells, are, so to speak, permeated by emanations of the matter 'si 12'. And when they have become sufficiently saturated the matter 'si 12' begins to crystallize. The crystallization of this matter constitutes the formation of the astral body.

OTHER EXAMPLES

Gurdjieff's belief that we are not all born with astral bodies but that they are acquired is debatable. On the reverse side of the coin, there is evidence that people who have not worked on themselves, who have never considered reaching their 'inner unity' unexpectedly find extensions of themselves.

Many victims of accidents who have had legs or arms amputated claim that they can sense the limbs and that the newly departed toes are itchy or missing fingers are aching. The medical profession explains that this is only the brain's sensory patterns which have not yet received the message of the amputation, but auric orientated psychics quite often see the aura of the missing limbs, and Kirlian photography has proved that dismembered plants still produce pictures of branches and leaves that are no longer part of them.

Russian scientists believe that the astral body exists. At the Kirov State Institute biochemists and biophysicists are using electron microscopes to study the possibilities of this ghostly, and as yet not totally explained, area of energy which seems to be part of us. They have got as far as concluding that the astral body is a form of biological plasma made up of ionized particles.

But who actually knows!

Eileen Garret, the medium, in her book *Awareness* states:

> Throughout all my life I have been aware of the fact that everyone possesses a second body – a double. The double is a distinct fact in Eastern and theosophical teaching and as such it is said to be an energy body, a magnetic area associated with the physical human corpus, an area in which the immaterial forces of the cosmos, the solar system, the planet and one's more immediate environment are normally transformed in the life and belief of the individual.

The British author, William Gerhardie (1895-1977) born and educated in St Petersburg, grew up in the less sceptical atmosphere of Russian society and in an account which appears in his *Resurrection*, he gives details of how he once woke up from a feverish sleep to realize that he was floating above his own body but attached to it by a shining cord running from the back of his neck to the forehead of his sleeping body. He was able to walk, though it was like wading through water.

A well-known actor and playwright and personal friend of

mine who, for years, has been practising various forms of psychic advancement told me about a very recent astral projection experience he went through. Low in spirits due to an imminent divorce, he lay down on his bed one evening and went through the various relaxing exercises he was in the habit of doing prior to attempting a projection. He very quickly felt himself lift off and out of his physical body. He decided to travel across London to see what his wife was doing – a touch of jealous curiosity playing a part in this. He entered the new apartment she was sharing with a girl friend, an apartment he had never been in before, found no difficulty in going through the front door like a ghost, and started down a dimly lit corridor.

Like Gerhardie, he said it was like wading through water, and he was also aware that his feet were at least twelve to fifteen inches *below* the surface of the uncarpeted floorboards.

Half way down the corridor he looked into a bedroom and was surprised to see it nicely furnished with a pair of bedside lamps that he had purchased shortly after he and his wife had got married. He felt 'somewhat miffed' that she had taken them without consulting him, but went on down the corridor aware that he could hear voices coming from another room.

The door was closed, but he eavesdropped. The conversation was not very audible and all he heard distinctly was his wife's friend saying, 'We'll have to throw it out and have it burned.'

On hearing the door knob turning, he panicked, had a very bad return journey, and awoke on his bed suffering from frightening palpitations.

Unsure whether he had actually projected or not, he rang up his wife.

'Say nothing, but just listen,' he told her. 'I have just visited you in a projection, you have got my blue bedside lamps in your bedroom, and your friend has decided to throw something out and have it burnt. Please confirm or deny.'

The wife, reluctant to believe her about-to-be *ex*-husband's psychic abilities reluctantly confirmed both points. A mattress was the subject under discussion in the room. Her friend's dog had got into the habit of sleeping on it and it was alive with fleas.

My friend, who had used his power of astral projection to spy, was of course taking a risk as anyone who tries experimenting projection takes a risk. It is however quite obviously very tempting to make use of such a power to benefit oneself.

A curious example is the account of one Ed Morrell, a prisoner in the Arizona State Penitentiary, who inadvertently found he could astrally project himself out of very uncomfortable situations. When prisoners were punished they were placed in canvas strait jackets which were then soaked in water so that when they dried they shrank, squeezing the person inside to an unbearable degree. Morrell found that while waiting for the slow shrinking to start, he could 'travel' outside his painful body, outside the prison walls and walk in the streets of San Francisco. The guards, annoyed that this particular prisoner seemed un-harmed after his punishment, reported him to the Governor who, after questioning Morrell and checking up on his stories of 'astral projection' eventually admitted that the man obviously had psychic abilities. The punishment was stopped, and Morrel found that he was unable to project himself without the fear of pain.

Was his astral projection triggered off subconsciously?

It appears so, though Geraldine Cummings, another well known British medium, does not think so.

Mind does not work directly on the brain. There is an etheric body which is the link between mind and the cells of the brain. Far more minute corpuscular particles than scientists are yet aware of travel along threads from the etheric body, or double, to certain regions of the body and to the brain. I might call them life units. This invisible body – called by men the double or unifying mechanism – is the only channel through which the mind and life may communicate with the physical shape. Should a thread snap between the two, there is immediately a failure in control.

A thread? Is it the silver thread seen by Gerhardie and mentioned again in an account by an American, Sylvan Muldoon, who, according to Colin Wilson, is the best known of all writers on the subject. He awoke one night when he was only twelve, with a feeling that he could not move, then realized that he was floating above his own body. He was attached to this physical body by a 'shining cord' which seemed to come out of the back of his neck.

THE ASTRAL PLANE

When discussing the art of astral projection with someone who has practised it for years I was warned from the very start, *'Do not attempt it without someone in attendance to give medical attention if needed.* The trouble does not start when you try to leave, it begins when you try to come back.'

An unpleasant description of what may happen is outlined in a book by Steve Richards entitled *The Traveller's Guide to the Astral Plane*:

> There is a tendency to panic during experiments, and if they reach an advanced state, the experimenter quickly finds there is *reason* to panic. He will try to get up out of the chair he is sitting in: his muscles will not obey him. His eyes will not open. His heartbeat cannot be felt. He has as it were re-entered a corpse. Gradually his vital processes begin to start up again, and his muscles, oxygen starved, go into violent convulsions. It is *extremely* important to maintain rigid self control during this phase, since these convulsions can be dangerous. They are, in any event, extraordinarily painful.

Before suggesting ways in which you can attempt to astrally project, it is also important to understand where you might go. The areas where the astral body may travel is known as the astral plane which, in simple terms, is a plane of another dimension. It is another world as real to us, in our waking state, as a dream, and as easy to forget. To travel there – before even contemplating visiting another part of the known physical world – one has to ascend through a series of levels by various ritual procedures which must be learned and practised.

The esoteric laws regarding astral projection of both Eastern and Western cultures is based on a knowledge of the astral planes and each religious foundation or order has different teachings on their particular views of the planes.

When a novice is initiated – a young Buddhist monk for example – he must first learn the rituals, the invocations, the names of his guides, the colours, scents and varied directions he will encounter on the planes along which he will travel.

Symbols are used in the teachings and the meaning of the symbols have to be understood as well as how the novice's conduct in the physical world may affect his journey.

There are 'pure' orders whose students choose to travel through goodness and hard work, but there are also perverse orders who delve into black magic rites so as to take short cuts to reach the same destination.

In all rituals, however, the object is to reach and explore that other dimension which has been described as, 'a tingling web of vibrations which sends ceaseless pulsations interweaving through the cosmos' (*The Encyclopedia of the Unexplained*) or, 'a region of exceeding brightness and full of creative potency'.

The geography of the astral plane has been mapped out for centuries in Eastern teachings. There are many descriptions of the planes which coincide with our ideas of both heaven and hell, of the world visited by the delirious, and that visited by those taking hallucinatory drugs. The three examples that follow are those which come nearest to what you could expect the astral planes to be like, should you choose to start on that journey.

From Lafcadio Hearn's *Gleanings in Buddha's Fields* comes this representation of one astral plane:

> The way rises from terrestrial conditions to other and superior worlds – passing first through the Six Heavens of Desire, then through the Seventeen Heavens of Form, and lastly through the Four Heavens of Formlessness, beyond which lies Nirvana.
>
> The requirements of physical life – the need of food, rest, and sexual relations – continue to be felt in the Heaven of Desire – which would seem to be higher physical worlds rather than what we commonly understand by the expression 'heavens'. Indeed, the conditions in

some of them are such as might be supposed to exist in planets more favoured than our own – in larger spheres warmed by a more genial sun. And some Buddhist texts actually place them in remote constellations – declaring that the Path leads from star to star, from galaxy to galaxy, from universe to universe, up to the limits of existence.

The Heavens of Desire are all heavens of sensuous life – heavens such as might answer to the dreams of artists and lovers and poets. But those who are able to traverse them without falling (and a fall, be it observed, is not difficult) pass into the supersensual Zone, first entering the Heavens of Luminous Observation of Existence and of Calm Meditation upon Existence. There are in number three – each higher than the preceding – and are named The Heaven of Sanctity, The Heaven of Higher Sanctity, and the Heaven of Great Sanctity. After these come the heavens known as the Heavens of Luminous Observation and Non-Existence and of Calm Mediation upon Non Existence. These are also three, and the names of them in order signify, Lesser Light, Light Unfathomable, and Light Making Sound, or, Light Sonorous. Here there is attained the highest degree of supersensuous joy possible to temporary conditions. Above are the states named the Heavens of Meditation of the Abandonment of Joy. The names of these states in their ascending order are, Lesser Purity, Purity Unfathomable, and Purity Supreme. In them neither joy nor pain, nor forceful feeling of any kind exist. There is a mild negative pleasure only – the pleasure of Heavenly Equanimity. Higher than these heavens are the eight spheres of Calm Meditation upon the Abandonment of all Joy and Pleasure. They are called the Cloudless, Holiness-Manifest, Vast Results, Empty of Name, Void of Heat, Fair-Appearing, Vision-Perfecting, and The Limit of Form. Herein pleasure and pain, and name and form, pass utterly away. But there remain ideas and thoughts.

He who can pass through these supersensuous realms enters at once into the spheres of Formlessness. These are four. In the first state all sense of individuality is lost. Even the thought of name and form becomes extinct, and there survives only the idea of Infinite Space, or Emptiness. In the second state this idea of space vanishes, and its place is filled by the Idea of Infinite Reason. But this idea of reason is anthropomorphic. It is an illusion, and it fades out in the third state, which is called the State-of-Nothing-to-take-hold-of. Here is only the Idea of Infinite Nothingness. But even this condition has been reached by the aid of the action of the personal mind. This action ceases. Then the fourth state is reached – state of 'neither namelessness-nor-not-namelessness'. Something of personal mentality continues to float vaguely here – the very uttermost expiring vibration of Karma – the last vanishing haze of Being. It melts, and the immeasurable revelation comes.

Thomas De Quincey (1785-1859) in his famous *Confessions of an Opium Eater* describes a journey into realms which many occultists have recognized as being the astral plane:

> I seemed to descend into chasms of sunless abysses, depths below depths, from which it seemed hopeless that I could ever reascend. Nor did I, by waking, feel that I had reascended. For indeed the state of gloom which attended these gorgeous spectacles, amounting at last to utter darkness, as of some suicidal despondency cannot be approached by words.
>
> There were. . .dreams of lakes and silvery expanses of water. The waters gradually changed their character – from translucent lakes, shining like mirrors, they became seas and oceans. And now came a tremendous change, which, unfolding itself slowly like a scroll, through many months, promised an abiding torment. Upon the rocking waters of the ocean the human face began to reveal itself. The sea appeared paved with innumerable faces, upturned to the heavens. Faces imploring, wrathful, despairing. Faces that surged upwards by thousands, by myriads, by generations. My mind tossed, as it seemed, upon the billowy ocean, and weltered upon the weltering waves.

This sighting of a myriad faces is quite often repeated in reports on the astral planes, figures, shadows, a land peopled with apparently formless characters who all the same communicate their existence.

Lastly, a more pleasant astral view, one of the hundreds of descriptions of a near-death experience, by an American railroad engineer who suffered an accident while at work on the lines – quoted from F.W.H. Myer's *Human Personality and its Survival of Bodily Death*.

> I saw a medium sized person standing at my right hand clothed in white with a bright countenance, beaming with intelligence. I knew

what he wanted in an instant, although he put his hand on my shoulder and said, 'Come with me.' We moved upward, and a little to the south-east, with the speed of lightning, as it were. I could see the hills, buildings, trees, and roads as we went up side by side until they vanished out of our sight. As we passed on, this glorious being that was with me told me he was going to show me the bright heavenly world. We soon came to a world of light and beauty, many thousand times larger than this earth, with at least four times as much light. The beauties of this place were beyond any human being to describe. I was seated by the tree of life on a square bench of what appeared to be green velvet moss, about eighteen inches high. There I saw many thousand spirits clothed in white and singing the heavenly songs. . .

Heaven obviously; the American railroad engineer was taken there by his archangel, you will say.

If you believe in heaven.

But such a description is repeated so often, and has been confirmed by those who have managed astral projection, that both the horror of De Quincey's opiate nightmare and the railroad engineer's paradise must be born in mind.

Why, then, a heavenly plain and a hellish one?

Helena Blavatsky had the simple answer.

In Theosophical terminology, the 'world of Boundless light' is known as Devachan. During every Devachan period (death or a visit to the astral plane?) the Ego (self) clothes itself with the reflection of the personality that was. The ideal efflorescence of all the eternal qualities, such as love and mercy, the love of the good, the true and beautiful, that ever spoke in the heart of the living personality clings to the Ego and therefore follows it to Devachan.

Hate and greed and deception, likewise, presumably also envelope the personality, if these exist in the traveller, so an astral hell is visited, in other words, the astral plane is a journey into the other you.

The Hindu system of astral projection is based on the theory that the physical body has a certain number of points through which the astral world enters. Each point is a network of vibrations referred to as 'wheels' or 'chakras' and the turning or conscious activity of these wheels enables what one might nowadays term 'lift off'.

The Jewish Cabala system enables the projectee to reach the astral plane by using the sefirotic tree if he works and concentrates hard on what he has to achieve.

The Cabalists believe that God created the universe through a complex juxtapositioning of ten sefiroth arranged diagrammatically in the shape of a tree which are on different world levels. To attain the astral plane one has to climb from the lowest to the highest sefira which represents virtues, vices, numbers, colours, deities, demons, plants, animals, each sefira being recognized by a symbol which must be understood by the traveller. Meditating among these symbols is essential: whatever path is taken has to be followed according to the rules or the journey can become not only pointless, but dangerous. Unexpected encounters have to be considered and the novice must at all times be prepared to meet unknown horrors. The astral body may receive fearful injuries and may even be torn apart and disintegrate in the process.

In the Tibetan rite of 'chod' or cutting, according to the *Encyclopedia of the Unexplained*.

'The highly trained adept invites elemental beings to feast on his body. It is a terrifying rite and the whole operation is carried out on the astral plane, and with full awareness on the part of the practitioner. It is always performed at night and alone, in a cremation ground, cemetery or other solitude where he is not likely to be disturbed. Slowly spirit forms appear in answer to the invitation, and one of them, usually a hideous demoness, advances on the adept with a sword, and cleaves his body apart, rips out his heart and viscera and rends his limbs. With cries of ghoulish triumph the other demons pounce on the victim, tear off pieces of his flesh and drink his blood. Throughout the feast the adept himself undergoes the agony of the sacrifice, for he feels all that is happening to him. When the spirits depart his astral body slowly returns to wholeness.'

ASTRAL PROJECTION STEP-BY-STEP

For a simpler and less painful do-it-yourself astral projection, you should induce a mood of total relaxation on yourself, as with any other psychic experiment, and lie down on a bed in a not too bright room, as comfortable as possible, warm, naked, your head propped up on a hard pillow so that you can see down the length of your body.

Stage 1   Keep your eyes wide open.

Stare at the ceiling.

Bring your eyes down slowly till the tips of your toes come into view.

Focus a yard or so beyond your toes.

Lock onto that space.

Stage 2   Close your eyes. Imagine yourself rising horizontally out of your body to a height of about two feet. Hold that image. Open your eyes, try to see your double and turn the double over.

Stage 3   Close your eyes.

Imagine yourself staring down at your own body, floating over it and slowly, very slowly moving down the length of your physical body, staring at your chin, your neck, your chest, your stomach, your pubic area, your thighs, knees, ankles, feet.

Imagine staring at your feet.

Holding that image pivot so that you see the *soles* of your feet.

Think hard about the soles of your feet as you pivot down and touch the floor at the end of the bed and *feel* the floor with the soles of your feet.

Stage 4   Imagine, hard, that you are going to open your eyes.

Ask your mind what your eyes will see?

Yourself lying full length on the bed, or yourself standing at the foot of the bed?

Whichever answer, be sure you have *one* clear image in your mind.

Stage 5   Open your eyes.

Ten to one you will get quite a shock at seeing the room from your bed as you always have.

Do not despair. You have imagined astral projection or you would not be disappointed.

Stage 6   Repeat Stage 1 to 5 again and again till you eventually open your eyes and see your physical body lying full length on the bed. Do not expect to be able to do this quickly. It takes a very long time to even get the feeling that you are disembodied, but it does eventually happen.

Go through the routine of 'lift off', turning, of setting down astrally at the foot of the bed and staring at yourself again and again.

Stage 7   When you are projected and can stare (at first with disbelief) at your own inert body, do not remain too long but prepare for the return journey. This should be done in reverse stages, slowly, calmly, imagining the soles of your feet, sensing lift off, floating over your physical body, turning over, gradually easing yourself down into your physical body and then opening your eyes when you feel the hard pillow against the back of your head, the sheets against the length of your body.

When you have achieved all these stages and have gained the confidence that you are capable of occupying the astral body and staring out from it, move your astral body stage by stage away from the foot of the bed. This cannot be done in one session, you have to have infinite patience, but each time you project yourself you should be able to do so further and further away each time.

173

When you manage to land your astral self ten or twelve feet away from your physical body and you are able to get back without any problems, then you should consider travelling farther afield, but beware of success which, for some, tends to excite and negate the newly acquired power.

Accidents in astral projection can be fatal if you are not prepared. While keeping your projection within your own room, apartment or house, presumably knowing who you are likely to see, the chances of shock are minimised, but if you venture out into the world beyond your own territory and your astral body is unexpectedly seen, reactions to it may trigger off a chain of events which you cannot control and you may inadvertently return too violently to the safety of your physical self, causing serious problems.

Normally your astral body cannot be seen by anyone else, nor can you see the reflection of your astral body in a mirror, but some clairvoyants will see your aura and perhaps your astral shape, and if they are innocent clairvoyants, that is persons who are unaware that they are psychic – shock may occur.

The danger to your astral body, therefore, is not tangible, you will not cut it on a jagged piece of wood, or tear it on a nail, but you might unsettle the confidence you have in it to a degree where you automatically return violently to your physical self, and a violent return is dangerous.

To end, as a warning, I reproduce the short passage from *Premonitions of an Inherited Mind* describing the return of an astral body. This account, though fictitious, is based on a true event when a friend who astrally projected herself requested me to be present in the room in case she needed help on her return.

The girl lay on the bed for about 45 minutes with no change in her physical condition, apparently peacefully asleep, before she curled up and turned on her side in a foetus position, which was quite normal. I actually did not think anything else would happen, deciding she had just dropped off, when after a further ten minutes, I saw a muscle in her arm twitch, like the nerve of a spider's dismembered leg.

Her fingers extended and she uncoiled until she was quite rigid in a spreadeagled position. Her whole being then started to vibrate as though an electric current were going through her.

Her whole frame then went into an extreme convulsion as though an outer force was taking hold of her and shaking her.

Then she went quite limp and stopped breathing.

At that moment I was terrified and approached her, unsure what to do.

Her eyes opened. She stared at the ceiling.

She was sweating, soaking.

She turned her head and saw me.

'God, I never want to do that again,' she said.

12
SEX AND THE OTHER YOU

In seeking the other you and practising psychic development, you are aiming at a transformation within yourself, a transmutation, an alchemy which makes demands on your physical and mental health. One question which continually crops up is 'Is sexual abstinence advisable for psychic development?'

The answer is no, rather the contrary.

Although Helena Blavatsky insisted that she was a virgin and total sexual abstinence was the only way to prepare oneself for paranormal activities she, with most religious orders, seems to be in a minority if one leans towards Eastern or more modern day doctrines. Eusepio Palladino, for one, tended to boast about her erotic tendencies and many a Victorian researcher in spiritualism discovered, to his horror, that mediums tended to play with their sexual inhibitions, whether they were genuine psychics or not, getting spirits to pinch or caress those parts of the human male that should not, in principle, be touched by strangers.

G.I. Gurdjieff was of the opinion that 'Sexual abstinence is necessary for transmutation only in certain cases, that is, for certain types of people. For others it is not at all necessary. And with yet others it comes by itself when transmutation begins. For certain types a long and complete sexual abstinence is necessary for transmutation to *begin*; this means in other words that without a long and complete sexual abstinence transmutation will not begin. But, once it has begun, abstinence is no longer necessary. In other cases, that is, with other types, transmutation can begin in normal sexual life – and, on the contrary, can begin sooner and proceed better with a very great outward expenditure of sex energy. In the third case, the beginning of transmutation does not require abstinence, but, having begun, transmutation takes the whole of sexual energy and puts an end to normal sexual life or the outward expenditure of sexual energy.'

Gurdjieff himself was very sexually orientated and, apart from having a number of children from different women, sometimes practised sexual telepathy. A woman who was sitting at a table next to Gurdjieff in a Paris restaurant one day became aware that he was staring at her, inhaling and exhaling in a rather strange way. Unable to take her eyes off him she then suddenly realized that 'I felt as though I had been struck right through my sexual centre!'

It is said that Gurdjieff was in this way capable of producing frequent orgasms in women.

TANTRISM

In Tantrism, the sex act is developed into several techniques to benefit those who search for paranormal advancement.

Tantrism is the oldest of the Indian religions and its basic philosophy is very similar to orthodox Buddhism and Hinduism.

Women are important in Tantrism and the belief by those who practise it that it is a superior religion to Buddhism and Hinduism, where the female is considered inferior, comes from the fact that they give women a very high status. Without women a man is not complete and cannot ascend to the desired psychic or physical heights. 'Women are the deities; women are life; women are ornaments. Be ever among women in thought,' is one of the

Tantrik teachings. 'Man is placed in a physical environment so that he may make use of it and benefit by the opportunities of advancement that it provides. He is given sensual appetites for the furtherance of his spiritual needs. The soul can only be saved through the body; that is why the soul has been provided with a physical vehicle in which its emancipation may be achieved. In reality, there is no antagonism between spirit and body, and for those who know how, the body can be made to serve the spirit.'

'The loss of semen,' according to A. Bharati on *The Tantrik Traditions*, 'is considered detrimental to all bodily, mental and spiritual powers, for semen contains the life force; it is the source of energy from which the spirit receives its sustenance. Semen stored in the body and properly utilized enhances all one's faculties and gives one great power. It is not the sexual climax but ejaculation that devitalizes the body and attenuates the soul. There are practices that produce prolonged orgasms without ejaculation, which are secrets of Tantrism and which are likened to ecstatic states of spiritual exaltation. True asceticism merely implies the building up of sexual tension, and then directing the built up energy into an internal circuit. Sexual desire is progressively heightened in Tantrik rites and thus, empowered by restraint, becomes a perennial fount of energy.'

Sexual energy undoubtedly plays a major part in psychic development, though whether it should be repressed or used to a point of ultimate exhaustion is still an uncharted area of the paranormal field. Certainly it is known that poltergeists are created by sexual energy, usually that emanating from unconscious disturbances in adolescent boys and girls.

In his book *The Imprisoned Splendour*, Rayner Johnson writes:

One of the most striking features of the poltergeist phenomena is that in an overwhelming majority of cases a young person seems to be the unconscious agent of the effects. In ninety-five per cent of cases it is a young girl; in five per cent a boy or youth. Moreover, sexual change or shock seems to be frequently associated either with the beginning

178

or the cessation of the phenomena. Puberty and adolescence are thus the periods favourable to the effects.

He also mentions the case of a young Australian medium who at the height of his wife's excitement in their early married life caused ornaments to fall off the mantelpiece.

So be warned.

SELF DISCOVERY AND PSYCHIC DEVELOPMENT

The discovery and successful use of the other you will depend on a total exploration of yourself – your mind, your body, and what you are able to do with both.

It will also depend on how capable you are of breaking down your inhibitions.

Psychic development is for the loner, the person who knows how to live by himself. It is a very personal and private business which can only be contemplated if you are either on your own or have access to plenty of time on your own. If you share your life with someone else you will find it very difficult to get the continuity of privacy over the long periods you need for most of the experiments and exercises mentioned.

If you are in love or sharing new areas of life with someone else, psychic development becomes virtually impossible. Though the emotion of love by no means belongs to the material world, the social demands of love are one hundred per cent of the material world, as are the demands made from any other shared excitement.

Where love (that is the devotion of one person for another) can play a part in psychic development is when the experimenter needs the help of someone he can trust, but this tends to be one sided, the experimenter leaving his or her partner once the experiment starts.

Psychic development, therefore, is partnerless.

You should be on your own from the start, selfish, egoistic, and sometimes self indulgent. You are unlikely to be a pleasant person to live with because you will not, in fact, be trying to be of this world, but very much of another. Sexual gratification attained alone is one of the quickest ways of getting to know yourself and negating all inhibitions, providing you are honest with yourself and admit it when you find pleasure in areas which your upbringing may have taught you are unacceptable.

Everything that you do in private should be acceptable to you. If it is not, because it repels, then the feeling of disgust too must be admitted and accepted.

In today's society we tend to be taught that the demands of our minds and the demands of our bodies are separate, that an intense sexual desire fired by pornography is physical, that an erotic dream comes only from the mind. This is not so. Our minds fuse continually with our bodies, our bodies fuse with our minds, and behind them both is the subconscious which you must reach and which is also fused with both mind and body.

To get to that subconsciousness you must break down all the barriers which have been set up by society, by your schooling, by religious teaching, by your parents. Inhibitions, which exist in all of us, cannot be allowed to hamper what you are striving for, and inhibitions are negated by total honesty.

Be dishonest with others if you must, but do not be dishonest with yourself.

Self deception is the enemy of the other you.

BIBLIOGRAPHY

Ash, M., *Health, Radiation & Healing*, Darton, Longman & Todd.

Baird, A.T., *One Hundred Cases of Survival After Death*, Werner Laurie, NY.

Barrett, Sir William, *Deathbed Visions*, 1926.

Bennett, Colin, *Practical Time Travel*, Samuel Weiser Inc., NY.

Blavatsky, H.P., *Isis Unveiled. The Secret Doctrine*, TPH.

Browning, N.L., *The Psychic World of Peter Hurkos*, Muller.

Bharati, A., *The Tantric Tradition*, Rider.

Buchanan, Joseph R., *Manual of Psychometry*, Boston, 1926.

Butler, W.E., *An Introduction to Telepathy*, Aquarian.
How to Develop Psychometry, Aquarian.
How to Develop Clairvoyancy, Aquarian.
How to Read the Aura, Aquarian.

Cannon, W.B., *Bodily Changes in Pain, Hunger, Fear & Rage*, Appleton, NY.

Carrington, Howard, *The American Seances with Eusepio Paladino*, NY, 1954.

Cavendish, Richard, (Editor), *The Encyclopedia of the Unexplained*, Routledge & Kegan Paul.

Chesterton, G.K., *Autobiography*, Penguin.

Cummins, Geraldine, *Unseen Adventures*, Rider.

Mind in Life and Death, Aquarian.

Swan on a Black Sea, Weiser.

Dasgupta, S.B., *An Introduction to Tantrik Buddhism*, Calcutta University Press.

Eddy, Mary Baker, *Science & Health*, Christian Science Publications.

Edwards, Harry, *Spirit Healing*, Jenkins.

Eisenbud, Jule, *The World of Ted Serios*, Morrow.

Eysenck, H.J., *The Uses & Abuses of Psychology*, Penguin.

Eysenck & Sarjent, *Explaining the Unexplained*, Weidenfeld & Nicholson.

Figuier, Guillaume, *Histoire du Merveilleux*, 1840.

Flammarion, Camille, *Des Forces Naturelles Inconnus*, (19th century).

Garrett, Eileen, *Awareness*, Putnam, NY.

Adventures in the Supernatural, Putnam, NY.

Many Voices, Putnam, NY.

Geller, Uri, *My Story*, Robson.

Guirdham, A., *The Nature of Healing*, Allen & Unwin.

Gurdjieff, G.I., *All and Everything*, Routledge & Kegan Paul.

Hearn, Lafcadio, *Gleanings in Buddha's Fields*, 1897.

Inglis, Brian, *The Paranormal*, Granada.

Natural and Supernatural, Granada.

Johnson, Raynor, *The Imprisoned Splendour*.

Leadbeater, C.W., *The Astral Plane*, TPH.

Messing, Wolf., *I Am a Telepathist*, Smena.

Myers, G., *Human Personality and Survival After Death*, 1904.

Nichols, Beverley, *Powers That Be*, Popular Library, NY.

Ostrander & Schroeder, *Psychic Discoveries Behind the Iron Curtain*, Abacus.

Ouspensky, P.D., *A New Model of the Universe*, Routledge & Kegan Paul.

In Search of the Miraculous, Routledge & Kegan Paul.

The Fourth Way, Routledge & Kegan Paul.

Tertium Organum, Routledge & Kegan Paul.

Psychology of Man's Possible Evolution, Routledge & Kegan Paul.

Owen, A.G., *Can We Explain the Poltergeist*, Garret Helix, NY.

Peters, F., *Boyhood with Gurdjieff*, Gollancz.

Powell, A.E., *The Astral Body*, TPH.

Pratt, J.G. & Roll, W.G., *The Seaford Disturbances*, Journal of Parapsychology.

Puharich, A., *Beyond Telepathy*, Doubleday, NY.

Rawson, P., *The Art of Tantra*, Thames & Hudson.

Rhine, J.B., *Extra Sensory Perception After Sixty Years*, Humphries, Boston.

Roll, W.G., *The Poltergeist*, Universe.

Rose, L., *Faith Healing*, Gollancz.

Richards, S., *Travellers Guide to the Astral Plane*, Aquarian.

Taylor, J., *Superminds*, Macdonald.

Waite, A.E., *The Pictorial Key to the Tarot*, Rider.

Walker, Benjamin, *Sex and The Supernatural*, Macdonald.

Watson, L., *The Romeo Error*, Coronet.

Supernature, Coronet.

Wilson, Colin, *The Occult*, Mayflower.

Mysteries, Granada.

The Psychic Detectives, Pan.

ACKNOWLEDGEMENTS

Acknowledgements are made to the following for granting permission to print extracts from the works listed below.

Granada Publishing Ltd for *The Panorama* by Brian Inglis.
Laurence Pollinger Ltd for *The World of Ted Serios* by Jule Eisenbud.
Routledge & Kegan Paul Ltd for *A New Model of the Universe, In Search of the Miraculous* by P.D. Ouspensky and *The Encyclopedia of the Unexplained*.
Thorson's Publishing Group Ltd for *The Traveller's Guide to the Astral Plain* by Steve Richards.

For the very few instances where our researchers have failed to find the holders of copyright we offer our apologies.

INDEX